HOW COUPLES CAN BUILD MARRIAGES THAT LAST FOREVER

UNBROKEN

PRAISE FOWOWE

For permissions requests, and enquiries about
UNBROKEN WORKSHOPS, **Contact:**
www.praisefowowedtech.com/unbroken
Email: admin@praisefowowedtech.com
Tel: +234 708 654 9834, +44 7960 813430, +18178817269

Praise Fowowe Research LLC
admin@praisefowowedtech.com
www.iampraisefowowe.com

Layout and Design: Creativia WebPro
Cover Design: Ayodeji Oluwadare
Copy Editor: Worital
Final Edit: Ronke Adeniyi

First Edition: November, 2024
Published by: Praise Fowowe International

Marriage | Relationships | Self-help.

DEDICATION

This book is dedicated to you, Oluwatosin Praise Fowowe, for selflessly embodying the principles within its pages and for patiently trusting the entire process of my research work. Your unwavering support and understanding have been my greatest blessings.

Nothing compares to the gift of a peaceful and loving spouse.

With all my love and gratitude.

Praise Fowowe

AKNOWLEGEMNET

This project represents more than just work; it embodies my passion and dedication. While it's impossible to mention everyone who contributed to bringing this vision to life, I am profoundly grateful to all involved, especially the amazing couples who allowed me to study their marriages. This has enabled the creation of the Family Systems Engineering framework, now used globally.

Central to my understanding of family life, the first acknowledgment must go to my mother. Her teachings on human relationships have been the bedrock of my journey. Thank you, Mum, my siblings, and our entire family for your unwavering love and support.

I extend my gratitude to my mother-in-law, Mrs. Arinola Afolabi, whose love and support have also immensely enriched my life.

Over the years, I have had the privilege to work with several groups whose contributions have been invaluable. My sincere thanks go to the Institute of Family Engineering and Development, the Network of Family Life Professionals Africa, House of Saviours leadership team and the Family Center Group.

Your trust in my service has been a great honor. Special appreciation goes to Ronke Adeniyi, who, even under challenging circumstances, went above and beyond to refine and perfect this book. Your diligence and attention to detail have been crucial. To my cousin Oluwaseun Alabi, thanks for pushing me beyond my known limit.

I am also grateful to the entire management team: Chidinma Nwobi, Zuriel Olowe, Ayodeji Lawrence, Aminah Yunus Alli, Motolani Abe, and Omotola Atitebi, who work tirelessly alongside me. Your collective efforts have been instrumental in this endeavor.

Running a complex organization demands exceptional support behind the scenes, and Motolani Abe-Falabi has been fundamental in ensuring smooth operations across all our activities as our group head. Your extraordinary commitment has not gone unnoticed. Additionally, I appreciate Bokun, who leads our operations in Europe, and my executive assistant, Maryjane, for your dedication and hard work. Thank you to Senge Layeefa for your invaluable media support services.

To the myriad of mentors, industry colleagues and ministry leaders and friends who have enriched my life, I owe you a debt of gratitude. Your guidance and wisdom have been a constant source of strength and inspiration.

I must appreciate the production team of Ossy Godson of Atmosphair Media Solutions, Folayemi of Worital and Ismail Bakare of Barky Press. Thanks for making this truly special.

Lastly, to my wife, my life partner, and our children, Oluwatosin, Tioluwanimi, and Imoleoluwa: thank you for allowing me the freedom to fully express my potential. You make family life a joyous journey. Your adaptability, corrective insights, and unwavering support have not only enhanced our family but also made me a better man.

I am forever grateful to God Almighty, who has entrusted me with the unique mission of transforming families across the globe through the family systems engineering framework.

TABLE OF CONTENT

INTRODUCTION

As I sit in my living room in Las Colinas, Irving, Texas, I'm enveloped by the serene beauty of nature—a muse that never fails to ignite my creative imagination. Outside my window, the dance of the swimming pool's waters captures my attention, while squirrels, my unlikely neighbors, glide effortlessly across the field. In these moments of tranquility, my thoughts often wander and today, they find themselves in the future of marriage—a concept both exciting and daunting in the age of the metaverse.

It was the notion of virtual unions that transported my mind back to the heart of my days AJ City in Lagos, Nigeria—a place where my research into the fabric of family life began. AJ City is a place of unpredictability, where Sunday mornings transform streets into football pitches, and evenings buzz with the camaraderie of local gatherings. Here, families of eleven might share a single room, yet when they step out, they carry an air of grace that looks nothing like their humble abode. It is located in the earth of Lagos state, the economic capital of the most populous black country in the world- Nigeria.

My time in AJ City was a chapter of rich experiences; from masquerading as a pastor who rescues young girls from the shadows of exploitation to seeking the wisdom of couples whose marriages were as enduring as the ancient baobab. These were the couples whose love had weathered quarter-century storms, still emerging with smiles that spoke of genuine contentment.

Born to an Anglican priest, my childhood was filled with different cultures, each move writing a question in my growing anthology of life. With no academic course in family science to quench my thirst for knowledge, it was the raw, unfiltered lessons from the field that became my classroom. In all of this, my academic pursuit was jolted into a personal quest by the tragedy of Mr. Dorime.

On that fateful, rain-soaked Sunday in AJ City, the Jacksons presented a portrait of marital bliss—united in step and spirit as they greeted their neighbors and swayed to the hymns of thanksgiving. None could have foreseen the sorrowful news that would later ripple through the streets: At exactly 5 pm, shocking news spread throughout the community. Mrs. Dorime had fatally stabbed her husband following the discovery of marital infidelity the previous day. My mind struggled to process the events as they unfolded, for her actions seemed inconceivable given the
calm demeanor I had witnessed earlier that day.

What, then, is the cornerstone of a truly happy, effective marriage?

This question took me on a journey of discovery, challenging the narratives spun by tradition and society. In a world rapidly morphing under the touch of technology, we yearn for a cornerstone of stability, a sanctuary of happiness. Such a foundation is paramount, for it is the harmonious union of two souls that can forge a society brimming with joy.

While the laws adapting to metaverse marriages remain shrouded in uncertainty, the essence of our humanity persists —we seek connection, companionship, and unity.

Whether through the avatars of the virtual world or the traditional bonds of wedlock, our quest for love remains unaltered. It is our duty, then, to craft a template for marriage that transcends boundaries, a blueprint for love that endures— an aspiration not just to dream but to achieve the marriage of our collective dreams.

CHAPTER 1

Why Did You Get Married?

They entered my office, a shadow of a couple once united in love, their eyes telling a story of countless futile attempts at mending what seemed irreparably broken. The air between them was thick with resignation—it was as if they had come to a funeral, not a session meant for rejuvenation.

I gestured towards the seats, signaling them to rest. In my years of guiding fractured marriages back to wholeness, I understood well that the disillusionment of a couple after five years paled in comparison to the deep-rooted disconnection of those bound for thirty-two.

The 'OYELA' assessment—a tool translating to *'Illumination'*—was my compass to navigate the puzzles of marital discord. Within ten minutes, it opened up layers of buried issues with startling clarity, and as I reviewed the results, I found myself holding onto a slender thread of hope amidst the desolation.

With a smile that could either provoke ire or inspire a release of long-carried burdens, I asked the question that has become my hallmark:

"Why Did You Get Married?"

Such a simple inquiry on the surface plunged the room into a profound silence that spanned over half an hour. They grappled with the elusive answer—a truth that should have been self-evident but now seemed as distant as a forgotten dream.

The truth eventually surfaced; thirty-two years of togetherness had yielded four thriving adults, yet they were unable to articulate the reason behind their union.

My inquiries dug deeper, utilizing the full extent of my expertise in neuro-linguistic programming and family systems engineering. We dug into the genesis of their marital strife which had begun in the wake of their nest emptying— when solitude echoed the absence of their last child.

This revelation led us to Janet's childhood in Kiev, in a home populated by the echoes of abandonment. As a favored child who helped the owner care for others, she found a semblance of purpose that followed her to adulthood, to college, and into the arms of Bruce.

It became clear that Janet's reason for marriage was rooted in her need to nurture. As the children arrived, her own life seemed to recede into the background, her identity dissolving into her role as a caregiver. Subconsciously, she had been filling a void left by her unfulfilled yearning for parental love—a void that parenting masked but never healed.

"Why this fervor for raising children?" I pressed on.

Janet had long awaited an apology from the parents who never came back—a silent hope that gnawed at her ability to accept love. In raising children, she convinced herself that her life's mission was to bestow the joy she never received onto others. And while she excelled in this self-appointed role, the absence of her children now reignited her suppressed pain.

Now, with her pain resurfacing and her narrative unravelling, Janet stood at a crossroads, ready to find new children in need of her love—a journey away from the marriage that could no longer contain her boundless maternal instinct.

******

WHOLENESS

In the heart of every effective couple, the habit of wholeness is found. This foundational principle suggests that the raw capacity to love, often dulled by life's injuries, can be rekindled. The most successful partners embrace the courage to confront their pain and assume responsibility for their healing, knowing that the health of their marriage is inextricably linked to their personal wholeness.

Through my work with numerous couples, I've discerned a recurring theme: unhealed pain, often masquerading as a coping mechanism, begins to seep out when those temporary fixes collapse.

As a child, I grappled with pain from early exposure to sexual abuse, which morphed into an addiction. This affliction was concealed behind a façade of problem-solving and dependability.

My refuge found in the shadows of sex and escapism was a ticking time bomb, bound to inflict harm. Loss compounded my suffering. The passing of three people close to me sent me into denial and depression. Acknowledging my pain seemed insurmountable, overshadowed by the fear of public perception. Yet, salvaging myself was essential to prevent further damage to those around me. This personal struggle allowed me to empathize deeply with Janet's plight and guide her toward the light of healing.

Processing Your Pains

We all harbor traumas, often shrouded in silence. Some of us cling to our pain as a way to gain attention, fearful that healing might extinguish the notice it brings. Others are paralyzed by the shame of discovery, keeping our suffering concealed within. Rationalization is a familiar refuge, but my two decades of family counselling have laid bare a truth: unprocessed pain is a silent saboteur of marriage.

Without confronting our pain, we risk wounding those we cherish and spiraling into a cycle of blame where our partner becomes the unwitting casualty of our unresolved conflicts.

If this book finds you in pain, consider its manifestations:
- A dwindling sexual desire.
- Irritation with your partner.
- Bursts of anger.
- A propensity for shouting or violence.
- An aversion to discussing your inner world,
- instead focusing on the flaws of others.
- Feelings of unlovableness, accompanied by a narrative that deems love overrated.

True connection in a relationship demands absolute vulnerability, a willingness to immerse yourself in your partner wholly. But first, you must process your pain.

ACTIVITY 1: **AUDITING THE HOUSE CALLED 'YOU'**

Imagine your life as a house, its structure reflective of your current state. Let's conduct an audit:

- **Foundation:** What experiences have laid the groundwork for your being?
- **Pillars:** What beliefs uphold your view of life, love, and the world?
- **Covering:** Who shelters you with wisdom and guidance?
- **Windows:** Do your relationships offer fresh air, or do they stifle you?
- **Painting:** How do perception and reality color your world?
- **Architect:** Does your life's design align with your divine purpose?
- **Client:** Are you, the dweller within, content with the house you've built?

Reflect on how these elements have shaped your capacity to love and be loved.

ACTIVITY 2: **PILGRIM'S AUDIT OF CHILDHOOD**

Embark on a pilgrimage to your past, seeking insights from those who knew you at pivotal life stages. Gather their memories of you and piece together a timeline of emotional milestones.

- Identify the pain points. Ask yourself, *"Why does this pain persist?"*
- Separate fact from fiction. What happened, and what didn't?
- Envision your life's trials as preparatory steps towards a greater purpose.

- If life's antagonists were but actors in your story, how well did they perform their roles?
- Who might you be destined to assist through your trials?
- Extract five lessons from your hardships. What now can this pain teach you?

Through this introspection, you're not just revisiting old wounds—you're transforming them into wisdom, redefining the narrative of your pain.

HABIT 1 – WHOLENESS

For many, the first habit of thriving couples might be a revelation: wholeness. It is the realization that the capacity to love, albeit raw and often subdued by life's harsh lessons, is innate in each of us. Effective couples have learned to confront their past pains, taking responsibility for their own healing—and in this journey toward wholeness, they find the keystone of a thriving marriage. One of the most challenging hurdles I've encountered in my life is my tendency to seek alternatives and not stay loyal to a group or person who has entered my life. It's as if I grow weary of connections after a while, including those I cherish. I couldn't quite grasp what was happening within me.

My initial reaction was to seek guidance through prayer and discussions with a few trusted mentors. Their insights were helpful, but the issue persisted. It became clear to me that I needed to embark on a deeper personal journey, recognizing that often, the path to the future resides in the past.

As I reflected on my behavioral patterns and upbringing, I uncovered a significant revelation. I attended three elementary schools and three secondary schools during my childhood. This nomadic lifestyle was a result of my father's frequent relocations as an Anglican priest. Each time I tried to settle in a new location and form close friendships, we were uprooted again. I never experienced closure with my best friends; instead, I was forced to start anew, building new relationships repeatedly. Unconsciously, this pattern had become ingrained in my psyche. I had unconsciously become skilled at having multiple best friends, depending on the circumstances. Strangely, this also affected my ability to bond deeply with my wife.

It took time, along with causing both myself and others pain, to recognize this pattern and its impact. I embarked on the challenging journey of learning how to achieve closure and determine who should occupy various tiers of friendship in my life: the outer court, inner court, and holiest of holies. This introspective exercise became instrumental in my quest for wholeness. Prior to this realization, whenever I felt hurt or discomfort, I instinctively sought new connections as temporary stopgaps. The constant underlying feeling was, *"I'll be moved to another location soon."*

Recognizing this was only the beginning. It took a heartrending journey through old wounds to learn the art of closure and to discern the concentric circles of relationships —from acquaintances to the sanctum of intimate friendships. This breakthrough was a turning point, shifting from a mindset braced for imminent goodbyes to one open to enduring connections. Such self-awareness is a cornerstone for many who, like me, have navigated through the murky waters of self-sabotage because it is in facing our shadows that our true light can finally shine forth, paving the way for a new reality.

I recognize that many of us grapple with self-sabotaging patterns that have been ingrained in us for years. Yet, we may not have taken the journey necessary to free ourselves from these patterns. It's vital that we confront our own darkness to allow our inner light to emerge. Only then can we begin creating a new reality that will shape our future?

Create Your Empowering Story

Neuro-Linguistic Programming posits that nothing possesses meaning except the meaning we ascribe to it. This tenet is for those seeking to redefine their past. Healing doesn't negate history; rather, it empowers us to reframe our stories, transforming pain into a force for personal and collective good.

What transpires in life and the narratives we construct can diverge significantly. Consider the man who interprets flat tyres as a nudge toward a new vehicle, while another sees it as a sign to halt his journey. Our interpretations are stories woven from the threads of our beliefs.

You may have experienced betrayal, tempting you to paint all with the same brush of distrust. Yet, another narrative is possible—one that acknowledges resilience and envisions past hurt as a crucible that forges a capacity to heal others. By viewing pain through the lens of empowerment, our perspective shifts, altering our emotional landscape and our reactions to the memories we hold.

Take Responsibility For Your New Outcomes Without Excuses

In crafting an innovative family life coaching framework, I studied couples married for over a quarter-century.

A common thread among them was the ownership of their individual journeys to wholeness. Such healing is integral to understanding the beauty of singleness and the synergy of partnership, where unity amplifies strengths without silencing individual passions.

Suppressing one's dreams for the sake of a partner's can be a silent killer of joy unless it's a choice made freely and reciprocally. Wholeness in both partners guards against this, leading to a marriage where both can flourish.

Wholeness is the bedrock upon which all other habits stand. It is the precursor to a union that is not just functional, but deeply fulfilling.

End Note Reflection Questions

Reflect on these questions with honesty and courage:

- Do I feel loved or unloved in my marriage? Why?
- Can I trace this feeling back to a moment or pattern in my past?
- When did I first sense a lack of love?
- What does being loved look like to me, and what steps can my spouse and I take to create this?
- What is my definition of love?
- Do I harbor self-love, truly?
- What are my views on gender equality, and how do they influence my relationship dynamics?
- How can I effectively communicate my need for love to my spouse?
- What signs or gestures could symbolize my need for connection, and how should my spouse respond?

In answering these questions, you embark on a path that not only illuminates your inner workings but also sets the stage for deeper intimacy and understanding in your marriage.

End note reflection questions

1. Personal Application:
- In what ways did the themes presented resonate with your personal experiences?
- Can you identify a moment in your life that parallels the journey or challenges discussed?

2. Challenges and Growth:
- What obstacles are you currently facing that the content has shed light on?

- How can the insights gained from this reading influence your approach to these challenges?

3. Change in Perspective:
- Has your perspective on any specific topic changed after reading? If so, in what way?
- What preconceptions did you have that have been challenged or affirmed?

4. Emotional Response:
- What emotions did you feel while reading, and what passages evoked the strongest response?
- How might these emotional responses guide your actions or decisions moving forward?

5. Actionable Steps:
- What are three actionable steps you can take immediately to apply the wisdom from this reading to your life?
- How will you measure the impact of these actions?

6. Knowledge Sharing:
- How would you explain the key takeaways from this reading to a friend or colleague?
- Is there a particular piece of knowledge from this reading that you feel compelled to share with others?

7. Further Inquiry:
- What questions have arisen for you that you wish to explore further?
- Are there topics discussed that you are now inspired to research or learn more about?

8. Integration into Daily Life:
- How can the principles or lessons from this reading be integrated into your daily habits or routines?
- In what ways might this integration improve your quality of life or relationships?

9. Long-Term Considerations:
- Considering the long-term impact, how might the insights from this reading influence your goals or plans for the future?
- What steps can you take to ensure that the lessons learned are not forgotten but instead contribute to your personal growth?

10. Reflective Creativity:
- If you were to create a piece of art, music, or writing inspired by this reading, what might it look like or communicate?
- How does engaging with your creative side help you process and internalize the information?

EMBRACE
GROWTH TOGETHER

> *Every challenge is an opportunity for growth. Embrace the journey of personal and relational development together, and let it strengthen your bond.*

CHAPTER 2

How Skilled Are You?

In the world of sports, some moments go beyond the game, and one such instance was the World Cup qualifier that would seal the fate of England or Greece for the 2002 finals. England, trailing behind, was teetering on the brink of a national disappointment at the storied Old Trafford.

It was a critical World Cup qualifier, the final match that would determine whether England or Greece would advance to the 2002 World Cup finals. England found themselves trailing 2-1, facing the grim prospect of ending the national footballing careers of some of their most esteemed icons.

Time seemed to slow down at Manchester United's Old Trafford stadium as the clock ticked toward the 3rd minute of stoppage time. Some fans had already started to leave, their hopes dashed, as it seemed almost impossible for England to turn the tide. All they needed was a draw to qualify, but their performance on the field hadn't shown any signs of a potential comeback.

Then, fate intervened. Teddy Sheringham was fouled, and it resulted in a free-kick opportunity, albeit from a distance where most players would consider a goal nearly impossible. But England had a secret weapon in their ranks, a skilled free-kick specialist, David Beckham. As the commentators would later say, "Cometh the hour, cometh the man." Even though his teammates and the crowd had little belief that a goal could be scored from such a challenging position, David Beckham remained undaunted his name synonymous with mastery over the ball. The stadium, a cauldron of nerves, stood on the precipice of despair and hope. He took his trademark steps toward the ball, exuding confidence, and expertly bent it like only he could. Every eye was fixated on the ball as it gracefully soared into the back of the net. With that stunning goal, England had equalized and secured their place in the World Cup. It was a moment that would go down in history as one of the most iconic and unforgettable in English national team football. It was a testament to the transformative power of skill—a processed talent brought to life in a critical moment.

HABIT 2: SKILLED DELIVERY

This story is a metaphor for marriage. Just as every player on that field could kick a ball, not all possess the refined skill to 'bend it like Beckham.' Similarly, marriage intertwines natural affinities with skills that must be learned and perfected.

During my Family Systems Engineering certification, I encountered a couple whose 48-year marriage was a testament to such skill. Their seamless bond and friendship sparked my curiosity—what was their secret?

The husband recounted a pivotal episode from their sixth year of marriage. His wife's withdrawal from intimacy had sparked a cycle of verbal abuse and threats, born out of frustration rather than understanding. Each sexual encounter left her feeling disrespected and unseen, a sentiment that had been silent for two years.

Listening to their story felt all too familiar, as I had encountered similar cases with my clients. These situations often boil down to one core issue: ineffective communication.

According to the wife's narrative, she had reached out to someone he deeply respected, a man who had essentially mentored him and taught him much about business. This man asked a simple question that had never crossed her husband's mind: Had he ever asked her how she wanted to be corrected or how she wanted to be loved? The answer was no. In his mind, he believed he held a superior position as a husband, and she should be content with whatever he did. This mindset had been shaped by the models of marriage he had seen while growing up.

After sharing the steps they took to overcome their challenges, which included seeking guidance on improving their sexual relationship and enrolling in a marital communication class, they left me with a profound statement I'll always remember: *"When all you have are talents, you will make a lot of noise but achieve so little. But when you subject your talents to processing and turn them into skills, you will achieve so much with ease, and life becomes simpler."*

Their journey highlighted the transformative power of effective communication and the importance of continuously working on oneself to enhance not only talents but also the skills that truly enrich life and relationships. In marriage, as in life, it's the development and application of skill that makes the difference between merely surviving and thriving.

Skills Bring Success

In many African cultures, Saturdays are festooned with wedding celebrations, often marked by lavish spending. Yet, despite the grandeur, numerous marriages quickly fold and things disintegrate. The reasons, though varied, are often traced to a common denominator: a deficit in marital skills. From effective communication to financial savviness, these are not just natural talents but abilities that must be honed.

When we delve into the reasons behind these failed marriages, we often encounter a familiar set of issues:
- Domestic violence
- Verbal abuse
- Financial stress
- Lack of sexual satisfaction
- Interference from in-laws
- Marital infidelity
- Marital stress

While these may seem like distinct problems, they can often be attributed to one common factor: low marital skills. People frequently make assumptions and enter marriage without having acquired the necessary skills.

For example, whilst talking may come naturally to some, effective communication is a skill that requires mastery. Earning money as a professional is one thing, but financial intelligence is a skill that must also be honed to prevent financial woes.

Whatever complaints your spouse may have can be seen as an essential to seek knowledge and apply it to overcome these challenges. While prayer has its place, some aspects of life require the pursuit of knowledge and its practical application for transformation.

The Christian holy book advises, "You shall know (knowledge) the truth, and the truth (applied) shall set you free."

EXERCISE: ASSESSING MARITAL SKILLS

As a couple, take a moment to evaluate each other's skills in the following areas on a scale from 0 (least) to 10 (most):

- Communication
- Sex & Romance
- Financial Intelligence
- Relationship Building
- Negotiation
- Organization
- Personal Appearance

Compare your scores to identify strengths and areas needing attention. This exercise isn't about judgment but about recognizing where growth can enrich your union. And while prayer and faith play their roles, they must walk hand in hand with actionable knowledge.

Foundations Often Conclude Histories

Typically, the areas of contention—those your partner often complains about—trace back to formative experiences.

Consider communication: its effectiveness is anchored in trust, perception, and connection. The upbringing influences these pillars significantly, shaping one's communication style.

Empathy serves as the bridge between different styles and leads to a deeper understanding.

A Divided World

In a society fragmented by ideologies and biases, the ability to listen and respond to your spouse's needs as they wish to be treated becomes even more critical. Prejudices and misconceptions can poison relationships just as they do communities.

Different communication styles exist, and it can be challenging for an intimidating communicator to connect with a creative communicator unless they step into each other's worlds to understand their unique perspectives. Empathy is often the bridge that connects people from different backgrounds and worldviews.

The world may sometimes perpetuate divisions, but children often view the world through innocent eyes. Our goal should be to preserve their unbiased view of humanity. Whatever areas your spouse may complain about are the areas where you urgently need to focus. Many people I've spoken to have sought help and developed the skills necessary for a joyful marriage.

For example, if sexual issues are a concern, consider implementing the "3-course meal order" approach. This method emphasizes asking your partner what they want and how they want it served, presenting it as requested, and awaiting feedback to ensure their satisfaction. Effective feedback skills are essential to avoid damaging the spirit of the relationship during these discussions.

Responding to Your Partner's Needs

If your partner voices a concern, it's a signal to examine that area closely. For instance, if intimacy is the issue, consider my '3 Course Meal Approach':

- **Preview:** Engage with your partner to understand their desires and preferences.
- **View:** Present intimacy in the way your partner enjoys, focusing on their experience.
- **Review:** Afterwards, openly discuss what was enjoyable and what could be better next time. Feedback is a skill in itself, crucial for continuous improvement.

Every issue flagged by your spouse is an opportunity for skill development, and often, acquiring these skills might involve seeking external help or education.

End Note Reflection Questions:

1. Reflect on a skill you wish to develop in response to your partner's needs. How do you plan to approach this learning process?

2. Think about the last time you and your partner had a disagreement. Which communication style did you employ, and how might empathy have altered the outcome?

3. In which areas do you feel most competent in your relationship, and how can these strengths be leveraged to support areas where you're less skilled?

4. How do the cultural narratives and societal divisions you've been exposed to influence your approach to your marriage and interactions with your spouse?

5. Discuss with your partner the concept of the '3 Course Meal Approach' to intimacy. What insights did you gain from each other's 'Preview, View, and Review'?

COMMUNICATION IS KEY

Open, honest communication forms the foundation of a strong marriage. Make space for each other to express thoughts, feelings, and needs without judgment.

CHAPTER 3

What Do You See? —Vision

Today was one of those wonderfully hectic days, for I had just completed a 14-day working visit to the United Kingdom. My journey had taken me through the beautiful, lively cities of London, Milton Keynes, and Manchester, as well as the serene town of Andover. Throughout my travels, I had the privilege of facilitating family life sessions and sharing the secrets of love and connection. The rolling greens of the countryside observed through the train window, became the canvas for my thoughts. It was here, amidst the laughter of young travelers and the tranquility of transit, that the essence of vision in marriage revealed itself to me anew.

As I reflect on this whirlwind experience, my heart swells with gratitude. The United Kingdom has left an indelible mark on my soul. I cannot help but smile as I recall the historic Old Trafford stadium in Manchester, where I had the honor of guiding a night session that stretched into the early hours. Exhausted but inspired, I cherished every moment.

However, amidst the excitement and busy schedules, I had momentarily set aside my manuscript, pausing the process of writing my book. You see, I believe in writing from the heart and forcing the words would never do justice to the message. The day was destined to offer a new twist. I was all set to fly to Edinburgh, Scotland, a first-time journey for me, but then came the message that my flight was canceled. With two essential sessions to facilitate, I couldn't afford to miss my commitments. So, I made a swift decision to embark on a five-hour train ride from London to Edinburgh. It was a journey I had not anticipated, but I found myself excited at the prospect of exploring the countryside.

As I settled into my train seat, my plan was simple: relax, perhaps catch up on some much-needed sleep, and let the miles roll by. However, destiny had other ideas. As the train glided through the picturesque countryside, the lush green fields and rolling hills ignited a spark of inspiration within me.

My gaze shifted to a group of seven lovely young ladies seated in front of me. Their laughter and youthful energy filled the carriage. It was at that moment that my mind began to race, recalling a powerful story from a couple I had met in my work, a couple who had shared the secret of a loving, enduring partnership.

This couple, with 51 years of marriage behind them, had faced their share of storms in the early years.

They had reached a point where their love alone couldn't carry them through, and they were contemplating parting ways. It was then that they decided to take a profound step – they chose to clarify their shared vision.

You see, in life, the wrong road can never lead to the right destination, regardless of how hard you try or pray. It's akin to embarking on a journey without a clear sense of where you are headed. In the case of this remarkable couple, their love was undeniable, but they had never aligned their individual visions of the future.

This story has become a pivotal part of my seminars worldwide because it highlights a fundamental truth: too many troubled marriages are a result of couples heading in different directions, believing love alone would guide them. Love is vital, yet understanding where you're headed together is equally crucial.

Imagine, for a moment, that both Joel and Jane had noble intentions for their family. Joel envisions creating a prosperous family that builds and passes on wealth through generations. Jane, on the other hand, aspires to nurture a godly family that radiates a sense of spiritual excellence wherever they go.

Both visions are admirable, but they are different destinations. A vision is essentially a mental image of a desired future. Joel's destination may resemble Sweden, while Jane's may be closer to Japan. So, while they both pour their love and efforts into their family, they are unknowingly pulling in opposite directions.

What follows is a subtle yet profound strain on their relationship. Both work tirelessly to fulfill their visions, often colliding because their paths diverge. This friction eventually leads to the term 'irreconcilable differences,' a phrase tragically associated with divorce.

Think about this question: Can you and your partner independently write down your family vision? Can you both articulate your aspirations for your family's future in identical words?

Many couples underestimate the power of a shared vision in building a harmonious family. As a family life innovator, I've seen complex family issues resolved simply by helping families define a shared vision, one that encompasses the aspirations of every member.

The couple I mentioned earlier, who had struggled with four wives and thirteen children, sought my guidance in rebuilding their fractured family. Within their household, seven different visions had emerged, leading to distrust and chaos. I convened a village meeting where each family member laid their cards on the table.

Through honest conversations and conflict-resolution sessions, we arrived at a unified vision that embraced everyone's aspirations. A year later, the family radiated mutual respect and love, with the walls of separation replaced by bridges of understanding.

The United States of America stands as a testament to the power of diverse individuals embracing a unified vision. Like the U.S., a family can thrive when it works collectively toward a shared goal.

Should The Husband Lead In Casting This Vision?

I know that conventional wisdom has often placed the responsibility of creating the family vision squarely on the shoulders of the husband. However, this perspective can sometimes overlook the valuable insights and aspirations that the wife brings to the table.

In truth, involving all major stakeholders in the process of vision casting is essential. Failing to do so can lead to unintended consequences, as any member of the family, regardless of gender, may have unique perspectives and dreams for their shared future.

In a family setting, leadership doesn't necessarily equate to being the smartest, wealthiest, or wisest. Instead, it means taking on the role of a servant-leader, someone who is dedicated to creating an ideal environment that promotes the best interests of everyone involved. This approach recognizes that each family member has a valuable role to play in shaping the family's destiny.

Unlike a nation where law enforcement can be employed to enforce a singular vision, families require thoughtful mediation and collaboration to achieve a win-win situation that respects and fulfills the aspirations of all its members.
In essence, leadership in the family is not autocratic but rather a call to serve, nurture, and unite everyone in pursuit of a shared and harmonious vision for the future.

Crafting a Powerful Family Vision: Uniting Hearts and Transforming Worlds

Within the complexity of family, there lies a potent force—the family vision. It's a compass that guides us through life's everchanging landscapes, a lighthouse in the darkest of storms, and a legacy that extends far beyond our years. A family vision isn't merely a statement; it's a testament to our collective identity, purpose, and impact.

Creating a strong family vision involves five pivotal elements, each weaving together to form a blend that resonates across cultures, beyond boundaries, and embraces the essence of humanity. These elements are more than just words; they are the roadmap to nurturing a family that not only flourishes but also positively influences the world.

1. Our Identity: The Birth of Unity

First, define your family's identity. Are you a tribe, a team, a village, or perhaps a company? Your chosen identity shapes the structure, culture, and values within your family. Let's consider a family that perceives itself as a team. In a team, individual roles complement each other, but the collective mission always takes precedence. Just as in a football game, where superstars alone don't secure victory, it's the unity and teamwork that prevail.

2. Our Identity Qualifier: Giving Clarity to Purpose

Identifying your family's identity is essential, but equally crucial is qualifying that identity. For instance, are you a team of loving friends or a village of innovators? Clarifying this aspect offers a precise vision that enables measurement. In our example, the vision may become: *"To build a team of loving friends."*

3. Unique Selling Proposition (USP): What Sets Us Apart

Every family carries something special—a Unique Selling Proposition (USP). It's that distinguishing feature that separates you from the rest. In a world of diversity, uniqueness shines. In our context, the team may choose "freedom" as their USP. This signifies that within this loving team, each member is free to be their authentic self—a place where no one needs to diminish for another to flourish.

4. Immediate Effect: Impact Beyond Ourselves

A powerful vision extends its reach beyond the family's boundaries. Who benefits from this identity, qualifier, and USP? Our vision must serve not only ourselves but also others. The goal isn't just to become number one but to improve the world around us. In this instance, we aim to uplift other winning families, multiplying the positive impact.

5. Ultimate Effect: Leaving a Legacy

Lastly, we contemplate the ultimate effect of our family vision. What happens when steps 1 through 4 are realized? Who will reap the ultimate rewards? A great vision extends beyond our own existence and creates a lasting legacy. Just as Israel's legacy has evolved from a family, your family's vision can shape your world. The United Arab Emirates is an astounding example of what a family's vision can do when they commit to transforming their nation and, consequently, the world.

In our case, the ultimate effect is nothing short of "transforming our world." It's a vision that leaves an indelible mark on society, shaping the future of countless lives and generations to come. Through these five elements, we unveil a vision that not only unites our family but radiates across cultures and generations, igniting positive change in the world. It's a vision that goes beyond boundaries, a legacy that endures, and a promise to transform lives—truly, a vision of a family for all.

Vision: The Light of Family Transformation

With a clear vision, a family gains a profound understanding of its collective journey, prompting a fundamental question: *"Who must we evolve into to manifest our shared dreams?"* This is where the real work begins, as it necessitates a transformation of who we are. One cannot cling to their current self while aspiring to manifest a new family vision. It's a common challenge, as many wish to usher in a new outcome while retaining their existing identity.

To address this, we employ what we call the *"Triangle of Life"* to unlock the necessary behavioral shifts required to realize our vision. Without aligning our conduct with the demands of our vision, our individual behavioral patterns can sabotage our collective aspirations.

Imagine, for a moment, a family with this vision: "To build a team of loving friends who are free to be themselves, raising other winning families, and transforming our world." Such a vision necessitates the elimination of competition, insecurity, and disrespect within the family. In this family, tantrums and tempers find no place, and conflicts are resolved amicably to encourage a win-win environment.

The Transformative Power of Vision

While some families have succeeded without a well-documented vision, embracing this practice enhances your chances of creating a transgenerational legacy. The adoption of a family vision brings about several transformative effects:

1. Vision Defines Your Family: A clear vision grants your family a unique identity, communicating your direction and aspirations. Just as no two nations are alike, your family's vision sets it apart from others.

2. Vision Refines Your Family: A well-defined vision transforms an emotional family into a structured system, refining individuals and elevating your family into a tribe that attracts others.

3. Vision Transforms Your Family: The power of a vision is its ability to shape your family, profoundly changing individuals. It's akin to witnessing the transformation of a raw gem into a polished jewel.

4. Vision Makes Your Life Intentional: Intentional living is paramount; it infuses life with purpose. Just as you wouldn't head to a train station without a destination in mind, a clear vision prepares and guides your journey.

5. Vision Eliminates Friction and Infighting: Families with uniform visions experience less conflict. When you have a shared destination, individual interests become harmonious.

6. Vision Promotes Purposeful Relationships: Vision alignment is vital in choosing the right spouse. Couples with aligned visions progress further and faster than those without.

7. Vision Helps You Leave a Legacy: Enduring organizations, empires, or nations always have a well-articulated vision. A vision-driven nation, like the United Arab Emirates, changes the lives of its citizens forever.

As the countryside rolls by, returning from Edinburgh's historic splendor, I am reminded of the unyielding power of vision. It's the architect of enduring edifices, the heart of homes that stand a century, the promise of a future sculpted by your hands.

You, too, can build something transcendent, a family that seeds a nation. The marriages that blossom are those rooted in a shared vision, an accord that becomes their very lexicon of love. Every thriving marriage possesses a mutually agreed-upon vision, illuminating the path to a shared legacy. Embrace the power of vision to guide your family's transformation, and watch as it unfolds a narrative of lasting significance.

PRIORITIZE QUALITY TIME

> *In the hustle and bustle of life, prioritize quality time together. Whether it's a date night or a quiet evening at home, cherish these moments of connection.*

CHAPTER 4

Winning Routines & Rituals: The Path to Success

Each day, for me, begins with the predawn whisper of 4:30am, an hour when the world is still draped in the shroud of night, yet my spirit awakens to embrace the day. This sacred ritual, unfailingly observed regardless of my global coordinates, is the cornerstone of my being. However, during the twilight of my UK sojourn, an unanticipated guest in the form of weakness waltzed into my life, challenging my steadfast routine.

Upon returning to the embrace of America's shores, I was greeted not by the familiar comfort of routine but by a mysterious ailment. Despite the armor of vaccination and a believed immunity carved through my odysseys in the pandemic stricken world, the reality was starkly different – I tested positive for COVID-19

In the face of this unforeseen adversary, I cloaked myself in the armor of calm and gratitude, reaching out to my beloved, miles away in Toronto, to share this twist in our tale. What followed was a solitary battle, a journey of introspection and healing, culminating in triumph within five days. But the battle left its scars – a lingering weakness that yearned to sway me away from the rhythm of my morning ritual.

As I stood before the bathroom mirror, the reflection I met was a reminder of the physical embodiment of my routine – a form that had danced through time, sculpted by discipline. The lethargy that sought to lead me astray was met with the resolve to return to my morning ballet – the ritual that defined my essence.

The Symphony of Shared Rituals in Love

In marriage, the couples we studied revealed a mesmerizing dance of routines and rituals. These practices, carefully choreographed, were the silent music to which their love stories pirouetted. In contrast, relationships that stumbled and fell often lacked this rhythm, the alignment of beliefs that is the undercurrent of enduring love. The absence of shared values often led individuals, who meant well individually, to inadvertently undermine their relationships.

...Values That Forge The Path to Routine Success

Take a moment to consider how professional boxers prepare for their bouts. The legendary Muhammad Ali's training regimen for the Thrilla in Manila documentary provides a striking example. His camp was situated far from loved ones, and every aspect of his life adhered to a meticulously planned schedule.

Another testament to the power of routines can be found in the life of Cristiano Ronaldo. He continued to play football when many of his contemporaries had retired or transitioned to punditry or coaching. Ronaldo's success was not solely due to his talent but also his creation of a routine and system that aligned every facet of his life with his desired outcomes.

Couples may dream together, envisioning a future painted in the hues of shared aspirations, yet it is the routine that brings these dreams to life. It is the brushstroke that turns vision into a vivid masterpiece of reality.

CONSIDER THE FOLLOWING INSIGHTS ON ROUTINES AND RITUALS

- **No Greatness Without a Great Routine:** Champions invariably follow an intentional routine. Anyone aspiring to be a world heavyweight boxing champion who spends their days sleeping, eating, and watching movies is either planning for self-destruction or eyeing an alternative career. Behind every champion's glory lies the unspoken tale of routine —the relentless practice, the unyielding discipline. It is the hidden architect of triumph.

- **Intentional Routines Prevent Accidental Success:** The power of prayer is often emphasized, but success is equally influenced by actions and thoughts. Effective routines include not just words but also thoughts and deeds. Routine is the rhythm to which success waltzes. Without this dance, success is but a fleeting shadow, a chance encounter rather than a destined embrace.

- **Routines Builds and Sustains Giants:** Couples often invest significant time together before marriage but subsequently abandon these activities after tying the knot. These shared experiences are what originally drew them close. Neglecting such routines can lead to relational stagnation. In love, as in life, routine is the kindling that keeps the fire burning. Couples must waltz to the music of shared activities that first drew them into each other's arms.

- **Routine Is the Path to Greatness:** Global icons who've fallen from grace often share a common trait — they discontinued the routines that propelled them to stardom. The story of Paul Gascoigne, a gifted English footballer, illustrates this all too well.

His career unraveled when he chose the bar over discipline. Your routine serves as a behavioral compass, guiding you toward your desired destination. When aligned with your goals, success becomes a natural consequence. Marriage, while dynamic, harbors numerous underlying structures within its ever-evolving dynamics.

Your routine serves as the code of conduct directing you toward your goals. However, understanding that success is more than a series of actions is paramount. While emotional intelligence garners significant attention, the emotional script aligning with your desired outcomes is equally vital. Marital gaps often exist beneath the surface, and couples who aspire to "build a tribe of loving friends who are free to be themselves, raising other winning families" must craft values and routines to translate their vision into reality.

Without adhering to these values and routines, a shared vision can remain a distant dream, and couples may find themselves adrift in a sea of unfulfilled potential. So, what are the routines you've let slip away?"

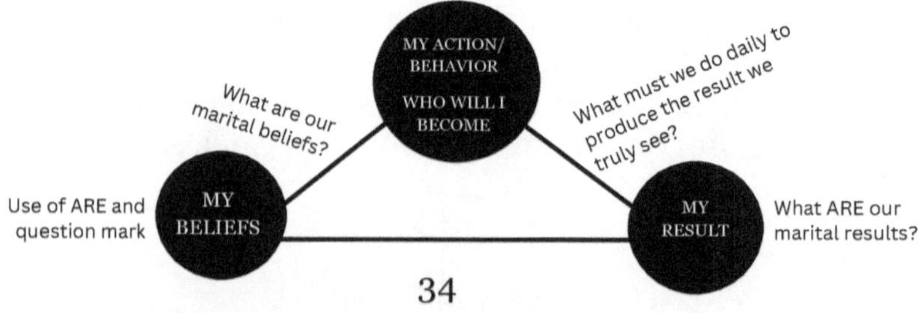

The third habit integral to building enduring and effective relationships is the seamless integration of values into the very systems and administrations of a couple's life together. This practice is akin to crafting a beautiful, complex fabric, where each thread represents a value, belief, or action, interwoven to create a stunning, cohesive picture.

The Blueprint of Marital Success

Think about the structure of a magnificent building: its strength and beauty lie not only in its design but also in the integrity of its foundations. Similarly, the outcomes you envision for your marriage are the architectural blueprints of your relationship.

These desired results become the cornerstone upon which every other element is built. In the diagram above the starting point is the predetermined end result you truly seek.

Once the blueprint is clear, the next crucial step is aligning your beliefs – these are the pillars that uphold the structure of your shared life. These beliefs must be consciously chosen and nurtured, sculpted to fit the unique form of the relationship you both aspire to cultivate. They are not just abstract concepts but active, living parts of your daily interactions. The beliefs must be strong enough to trigger the actions that can deliver your desired results.

Actions Speak Louder: The Art of Habitual Harmony

The most critical aspect, however, is the action – the habits you cultivate and the rituals you perform. These are the bricks and mortar of your relationship, the tangible expressions of your shared values and beliefs. Your actions are a direct reflection of the future you are building together. They are the daily strokes of paint on the canvas of your marriage.

Show me the actions and habits that you both engage in, and I can paint a picture of the marital future that awaits you. Like a skilled artist who can predict the final image from the first few brushstrokes, the habits you form reveal the masterpiece of your relationship that is slowly taking shape.

The Symphony of Shared Values

Imagine your relationship as a symphony – each value and action is a note, each belief a chord. When these are played in harmony, they create a melody that resonates with the rhythm of your shared aspirations. But if these notes are discordant if they clash and jangle, the music of your relationship becomes chaotic and unsettling.

In integrating values into your relationship, consider them as the instruments in your symphonic arsenal. Select them with care, tune them with intention, and play them with passion and precision. Let the music you create together be a reflection of the world you wish to build – a world where harmony, understanding, and shared purpose are the melodies that guide your days.

Vision Is Not Enough...

The previous chapter illuminated the crafting of a family vision – a light guiding the path of a relationship. Yet, as we go further in our journey, we encounter an essential truth: vision alone is not sufficient. A vision without an implementation strategy is like a ship with a destination but no compass or sails. It's a dream adrift in the sea of potential, yearning for the winds of action to breathe life into its sails.

The Bridge From Vision To Reality

1. Crafting the Implementation Strategy:
- Think of your vision as a distant star in the night sky – beautiful and inspiring, yet seemingly out of reach.

The implementation strategy is the rocket that propels you toward that star. It's a detailed, step-by-step plan that outlines how you will bring your vision to life. This plan should be as concrete and specific as possible, breaking down the vision into achievable tasks and milestones.

2. Setting Realistic Goals and Timelines:

- Each goal you set should be a rung on the ladder leading to your vision. These goals must be realistic and timebound. Consider what can be achieved daily, weekly, monthly, and annually. By setting these timelines, you create a sense of urgency and progress, transforming the intangible into tangible achievements.

3. Regular Reviews and Adjustments:

- The path to realizing a vision is rarely a straight line. It requires constant navigation and sometimes, recalibration. Schedule regular reviews of your progress. During these sessions, be honest about what's working and what's not. This is not an exercise in self-critique but an opportunity for growth and adjustment.

4. Building a Supportive Environment:

- Surround yourself with people who support and believe in your vision. This support network can be a source of encouragement, advice, and sometimes, constructive criticism. Remember, the journey to achieving a vision is often enriched through shared experiences and insights.

5. Celebrating Milestones:

- Acknowledge and celebrate each milestone you achieve. These celebrations are not just markers of progress but also moments of gratitude and motivation. They serve as reminders of how far you've come and fuel for how far you still have to go.

Embracing the Symphony of Implementation

Imagine your journey of implementation as a symphony. Each step, each task, and each achieved goal is a note played in this grand musical piece. Some notes might be sharp, others flat, but together, they compose the melody of your journey. This symphony is not just about the end but also about the beauty and learning in the process of getting there.

In the words of Jumai and Peter Foster:

"When we got married, we had our initial meeting and decided to apply my accounting practice to understand the assets and liabilities we had brought into our marriage. It immediately became clear that Peter had experienced a better family upbringing than I did. His family was known for building a fantastic marriage filled with love and togetherness, while my family's dynamics were neither notably good nor bad during my upbringing.

We quickly made the decision to interview Peter's parents, which revealed something quite astonishing. Apparently, there was a family ritual in their household, where parents shared the critical pillars for their successful family life with their children once they reached the age of 17. However, this ritual had fallen by the wayside in the younger generation, as they began to embrace modern trends and believed that young people should be allowed
to live their lives without interference.

Little did they know that they were on the verge of abandoning a tradition that had served generations so successfully. That initial meeting turned out to be a lifeline for us. Peter's parents sat us down and walked us through the ritual of creating our family vision, values, and what they referred to as the 'mythology' of what we wanted to create in our family. In my teachings, we refer to these as family legends.

Crafting these intentional systems made our marriage journey incredibly smooth because we were both fully committed to them. As our family grew with the arrival of children, they encountered a well-established and harmonious system that nurtured their growth. The beauty of it all was that we never forgot to pass this wisdom down to our own children.

Now, 47 years into our journey of intentionality, as you may have noticed, we have not only kept our friendship intact but have also seen the fruits of our commitment to the harmonious and thriving family life we've created." - Jumai

Jumai and Peter Foster's story is a vibrant example of cultural and religious integration, beautifully woven into a harmonious family system. Their journey defies the often-held stereotypes surrounding inter-religious marriages, showcasing the potential for unity in diversity. Their story is one of those stories I am never tired of sharing.

The Elements of an Effective Family System

To construct a robust and effective family system, couples must embark on a journey of intentional creation, weaving together the following elements:

A. The Family Vision:
- This is your family's North Star, guiding you through the journey of life. It should reflect not just your aspirations but also the essence of who you are as a unit. It's a vision that transcends the ordinary, bridging gaps and uniting differences.

B. The Family Values:
- These are the pillars upon which your family stands. Values are more than moral compasses; they are the

heartbeat of your family's ethos. In crafting these values, it's crucial to transcend biases and converge on principles that genuinely resonate with your shared vision.

C. The DNA Creed of Your Family:
- This is the unique genetic code of your family's identity. Just as DNA is unique to each individual, your family's creed is a distinct combination of beliefs, traditions, and practices that define your collective identity.

D. The Family Legends:
- These are the stories that shape your family's narrative. They are tales of triumphs, challenges, and milestones that become the folklore of your family, passed down through generations, knitting together your past, present, and future.

E. The Family Constitution:
- This encompasses the ideology and the governing principles of your family. It's a manifesto that outlines how you operate, make decisions, and navigate the complexities of life as a unit.

Navigating The Process.

The journey to establishing these elements is not merely an academic exercise. It's a deep dive into the core of what makes a family not just function, but thrive and leave a legacy. In my workshops, couples often find crafting their family vision a transformative experience. It's a process of discovery, alignment, and commitment.

When it comes to establishing family values, the challenge is often in breaking free from the mold of societal or religious norms and truly reflecting on what values serve your family's unique vision. It's about finding a balance between external influences and your inner truths.

For instance, a couple aspiring to be "fun merchants of the world" might initially list values like integrity, excellence, holiness, righteousness, and godliness. While commendable, these values might not fully resonate with their vision. It's essential to scrutinize and ensure that your values are not just admirable but also aligned with your family's goals and identity.

The questions I often ask here as a family life consultant are:
- Can you be godly without being holy?
- Can you be holy without having integrity?
- Can you have integrity without being righteous?

Values: The Heartbeat of Your Family Nation

In constructing the fabric of your family nation, the process of defining values is akin to laying down the foundational stones of an ancient civilization. It's about crafting a culture that not only resonates with your vision but also becomes the heartbeat of your family's unique identity. Jumai and Peter Foster's approach underlines the importance of aligning values not merely with religious or societal norms, but with the vision you earnestly seek for your family.

Building Values That Echo Your Vision

1. The Synthesis of Vision and Values:
- The Fosters' case exemplifies the need for values that directly support and amplify their vision. Values like fun, excellence, innovation, integrity, and leadership become the pillars upon which their vision of being "fun merchants of the world" is built. These values don't just adorn their family's ethos; they are the lifeblood that courses through it, making the vision attainable and real.

2. The Values Structure: A Step-by-Step Guide

Step 1: Visualize Through the Triangle of Life:
- Imagine your vision at the base of a triangle. Discuss with your partner as if you are consultants tasked with crafting the core values of a nascent nation. This exercise elevates your perspective, encouraging a broader and more creative approach.

Step 2: Brainstorming Values and Attributes:
- List attributes that resonate with your vision. What traits would the citizens of this envisioned nation embody? Be expansive and imaginative in this process.

Step 3: Selecting Top Attributes:
- From your list, choose five attributes that align with the following categories, ensuring they collectively drive your vision forward:

1. Personal Development Outcome: A value that propels personal growth and competence.
2. Human Relationship Outcome: A value that guides interactions within the family, such as kindness.
3. Unique Selling Proposition Outcome: A value that distinctively aligns with and highlights your family's vision.
4. External Engagement Outcome: A value that defines your family's interaction with the wider world.
5. Wholeness and Spirituality Outcome: A value that reflects your family's inner beliefs and spiritual alignment.

Step 4: Validating Values Against Vision:
- Critically assess if these selected values, when lived out, can genuinely lead to the realization of your vision. This is a litmus test for their efficacy.

Step 5: Crafting Your DNA Creed:
- Transform your values into a DNA creed. This creed is a declaration of your family's culture and ethos, a guiding manifesto that dictates behaviors and interactions.

Step 6: Weaving the Family Legends:
- Create a compelling narrative that becomes your family's legend, passed down through generations. This story encapsulates the essence of your family's values and vision, solidifying the identity you're building.

Let us examine the following example:

Sonia and Ike: Building a Family of World-Changers Sonia and Ike's story is a beautiful illustration of how a family, bound by shared values and a powerful vision, can become a source of hope and transformation in society. Their journey from envisioning to embodying their family's creed provides a template for families seeking to make a tangible impact in the world.

The Embodiment of Vision and Values
Sonia and Ike have laid the foundation of a family destined to influence and inspire.

Their vision,
"We are a tribe of influencers creating innovative solutions that transform our society in service to God and humanity."

Their vision is not just a statement but a commitment to a way of living that transcends the ordinary. It's a promise to be agents of change, to serve a purpose greater than themselves.

The Pillars of Their Family Nation

Their values –
- Trustworthiness
- Worship
- Influence
- Responsibility
- Love

These are the pillars upon which their family nation stands. Each value is a commitment, a guiding principle that shapes how they interact with each other and the world:

- **Trustworthiness:** In their tribe, every word, and every action is a testament to reliability and integrity.
- **Worship:** Their actions and lives are offerings, a way to honor their faith and beliefs.
- **Influence:** They strive to be role models, setting a standard of excellence and innovation.
- **Responsibility:** Sonia and Ike instill a sense of stewardship in their family – for each other, their community, and the world.
- **Love:** At the core of their family is love – a force that binds, heals, and uplifts.

The DNA Creed: A Manifesto of Their Essence

We belong to a tribe of Saviors and are Trustworthy. Whatever goes out of us must pass the test of WORSHIP unto God.
We INFLUENCE our world with superior lifestyle and solutions everywhere we go and we take RESPONSIBILITY for what happens in and around us.
We are LOVE and heaven is what you experience when you encounter us. WE ARE SAVIORS & we create solutions for our world.

The Legend That Drives Them

The Legend of The Solution Seekers

In a time when the world faced unprecedented challenges, a period known as the "Post-Covid Era," darkness seemed to engulf the Earth. Global crises, from the aftermath of the 2020 pandemic to the rise of extremism and ideological clashes, cast a long shadow over humanity. It was as if the very foundations of society were trembling, and the world was desperate for change. As the news media resonated with turmoil and uncertainty, a glimmer of hope emerged from an unexpected source—the union of two extraordinary souls, Sonia and Ike. Their love story was not just one of hearts intertwined but of a shared vision to mend the fractures of a fractured world.

Sonia and Ike, driven by a strong faith in God and an unquenchable love for humanity, embarked on a mission to build not just a family but a tribe of influencers—The Solution Seekers. They believed in a simple yet profound idea: that love, innovation, and service could heal the wounds of the world. Their commitment was steady, their determination unyielding. Together, they sowed the seeds of transformation, and their family became the torchbearers of this noble legacy. Every member of their family was nurtured to become a Solution Provider, armed not with weapons but with ideas, compassion, and a relentless pursuit of solutions to the world's most pressing problems.

Across the generations, the family thrived, and the legend grew stronger. They became known not for their wealth or power, but for their steadfast commitment to humanity. Their legacy was one of innovation, compassion, and unity, where differences were celebrated, and love was the universal language. The Solution Seekers, as they came to be known, inspired generations to transcend boundaries, think beyond themselves, and dedicate their lives to making the world a better place. They didn't just talk about change;

they were the change. Their actions echoed the belief that together, we could overcome any challenge, bridge any divide, and bring forth a world where love, innovation, and service were the guiding lights.

And so, descendants of this remarkable family, remember your roots and the legend of The Solution Seekers. As you walk through life's journey, may you carry the torch of love, innovation, and service high. Let it be known that you are part of a lineage that didn't just dream of transforming the world; they lived it, breathed it, and made it a reality. Let their legacy be your inspiration, your guiding star, and your call to action. Together, may you continue to illuminate the path towards a better world for all, in service to God and humanity

Reflection Questions:

1. How does the vision of Sonia and Ike resonate with your understanding of a family's role in society?

2. Reflect on their values. How do they collectively work towards achieving their vision?

3. Consider the DNA creed of Sonia and Ike's family. How does this creed shape their daily actions and decisions?

4. Think about the legend of their family. How does having such a narrative influence the identity and purpose of family members?

5. If you were to create a similar legend for your family, what key elements from your family's vision and values would you include?

CHAPTER 5

The Big WHY Habit

The Big WHY Habit: Discovering Purpose Together

The year 2000 marked a pivotal chapter in my life, one that would shape my understanding of purpose and its profound impact on relationships. Posted to the Northeastern part of Nigeria for the national youth service program, I embarked on an 18-hour journey from Lagos State. It was a journey into the unknown, filled with curiosity and a desire to make a meaningful impact.

Embracing Diversity and Finding Purpose
Arriving at the orientation camp, I was greeted by a diverse crowd representing the rich heritage of Nigeria's multi-ethnic society.

The camp, under the stern watch of Lt. Col Mukjah Kpero, was a melting pot of cultures and perspectives. It was here, amidst the rigorous para-military drills and the ever-busy life of the camp, that I began to truly appreciate the diversity of my country – a diversity that was both a strength and a challenge.

The orientation camp was an exhilarating experience, as we were divided into different platoons and subjected to daily paramilitary drills. Thanks to my past experience with the Boys Brigade parade during my formative years, I emerged as the platoon leader. The camp was a microcosm of society, where we encountered individuals from all walks of life, ranging from the good to the bad and the ugly.

Religiously, there was a vibrant Christian community under the banner of the Nigerian Christian Corps Fellowship, which held daily gatherings. Additionally, there were other Christian denominations, each with its unique identity and preferences. The Muslim community also had its various groups and activities. However, one place that brought everyone together was the legendary *"Mammy Market."*

The Mammy Market: A Microcosm of Life's Complexities

The Mammy market, with its lively atmosphere, was a hub ofcamp life. Beyond being a place for snacks and local cuisine, it was a place where the complexities of human relationships unfolded – a place of mingled stories, some wholesome, others less so. It served as a reminder of the myriad of choices that define our paths.

Mammy Market was essentially the military's version of a Walmart store, albeit in an open-air setting. Here, you could purchase snacks and meals from local eateries, which were a welcome supplement to the sometimes questionably prepared mass-produced food served to us *"bloody corpers."*

But Mammy Market had a reputation beyond its culinary offerings. It was rumored to be a place where "accidental lovers" found each other for discreet rendezvous. Indeed, there were unsettling stories of married individuals temporarily forsaking their marital vows during our four-week camp stay.

My daily routine in camp was straightforward, as I revolved around a triangular life consisting of my living quarters, the parade ground, and the Christian Fellowship. At the fellowship, I volunteered to play music and sing, drawing from my background as an organist at the Anglican church, where my father led the congregation.

Unexpectedly, the Christian Fellowship began selecting leaders annually to oversee the organization at the state level. I had never considered this role, as my heart was set on venturing to a remote village near the Cameroonian border to make a positive impact on the lives of young people in that region. However, fate had other plans. When the leadership list was revealed, I was appointed as the State Music Director for the year. Initially, I was determined to decline the position, believing it was not in line with my personal aspirations. However, I was presented with a 24-hour window to reconsider my decision. Ultimately, I reluctantly accepted the role, despite my initial intentions to decline it.

A Book That Changed Everything

In the midst of this bustling environment, a chance encounter with Dr. Myles Munroe's book, *"Maximizing Your Potentials,"* changed everything. The book, which I initially picked up out of casual interest, opened my eyes to the concept of purpose – the big WHY in life. Dr. Munroe's profound statement, *"When purpose is not discovered, abuse is inevitable,"* resonated deeply with me. It was a revelation that purpose isn't just an individual pursuit but a critical component of successful relationships, especially marriage.

WHAT IS YOUR WHY?

The Big WHY in Marriage

The most effective couples, I learned, are those who share a big WHY – a common purpose that drives their union. This shared purpose is the anchor that holds them steady through life's storms and the compass that guides their joint decisions and actions. It's more than just shared interests or compatible personalities; it's about aligning their deepest values and aspirations.

The most effective couples are all people of the big why?

The Essence of WHY: Opening the Core of Marriage

The concept of 'why' in marriage is more than the superficial layers of attraction and compatibility, delving into the profound depths of purpose and intention. This chapter explores the critical importance of understanding the underlying 'why' in a marriage, a concept that often determines the resilience and longevity of the union.

In a world that often glorifies scandal and betrayal, a remarkable tale emerged - one that would resonate across continents and generations, leaving a remarkable difference in the essence of marriage.

It all began with the revelation of a celebrated global leader's affair with an intern, an affair that threatened to shatter not only his career but the very fabric of his marriage. The world held its breath, waiting for his wife's inevitable departure, a decision most expected as natural in such a circumstance. However, in a moment that stunned humanity, she chose to stand firmly by her husband's side. Years later, when asked about her decision, she offered words of wisdom that would echo through eternity:

"When infidelity came knocking, the purpose for which we joined in matrimony stood as a towering light, untouched by the sting of adultery."

In this narrative, we pass time and continents to arrive at a coaching session with my very first clients, Richard and Kate, residing in the heart of Australia. Their marriage teetered on the precipice of dissolution, the term *"irreconcilable differences"* hovering ominously over their heads.

Kate, in a moment of despair, confided in her mother, who, serendipitously, had been following my inspirational YouTube series. Recognizing the depth of her daughter's despair, Kate's mother recommended that she reach out to me. An extensive email, heavy with the weight of her troubles, landed in my inbox, a cry for help amidst the gloom.

While many may have advised her to proceed with the divorce, my response was different. I proposed a marital assessment, a comprehensive analysis of their relationship dynamics, which I had developed over two years. Richard and Kate, willing to give it one last chance, undertook the psychometric evaluation, the results of which left them astounded by its accuracy.

The journey of revelation commenced during our coaching sessions, as it often does. However, it was a single, profound question that laid bare the root of their problems, a question whose answer eludes countless couples:

"Why Did You Get Married?"

To their astonishment, they discovered they had never truly addressed this question before walking down the aisle. Their responses, upon introspection, appeared selfish, devoid of any genuine intent to enhance the other's life. In this tale of troubled marriages, it becomes evident that the most fundamental questions often remain unasked and unanswered.

The ease with which couples press the exit button when faced with adversity is a testament to this lack of profound understanding and shared purpose in marriage. It begs the question: How often have you encountered reasons such as these for entering matrimony?

- "I married for someone to care for our home."
- "I married because of physical attraction."
- "I married due to sexual compatibility."
- "I married because I believed my partner would provide for me."

When the cost of drifting apart holds no significant consequence, the purpose itself is rendered fragile and incapable of withstanding life's tempests. It is not a call to advocate for staying in a marriage at all costs, for that decision rests solely with those involved. Rather, it underscores a recurring pattern where the original purpose for marriage proves too feeble to endure challenges.

As a family life strategist with decades of experience, I have posed a hypothetical question to countless couples on the brink of separation: "What if staying married for 40 years meant inheriting the entirety of China's economy, including its treasury?"

A staggering 89% of respondents expressed a willingness to do whatever it took, even seeking help to overcome their self-sabotaging behaviors, to inherit such a prize. It becomes evident that couples driven by a higher purpose are motivated to collaborate tirelessly, transforming their family into a clan and eventually a tribe, realizing that families from history burgeoned into empires and nations. We often underestimate the potential within our families when we fail to adopt a systems-driven approach to attain predictable outcomes.

In a world where people often enter a lifelong partnership based on physical attributes or fleeting desires, the moment a marriage's true purpose remains undeciphered and unarticulated, couples unwittingly work against themselves, attributing their troubles to "irreconcilable differences." It is in the unveiling of a shared purpose that the foundations of a lasting union are laid.

Why on earth would someone walk into what should be a lifetime partnership with someone who only chose you because of the shape of your body or the quality of your kiss? Truth is the moment the purpose for getting married is not deciphered and clearly articulated many couples will work against themselves and blame it on irreconcilable differences.

Reflecting On The WHY

1. Understanding the Real WHY:
- Couples need to introspectively assess the real reasons behind their decision to marry. This understanding forms the bedrock of their relationship, giving it the strength to endure challenges.

2. Beyond Superficial Reasons:
- Marriages based on superficial reasons like physical attraction or financial benefits lack the depth to sustain long-term commitment and growth.

3. The Power of a Shared Purpose:
- When couples share a higher purpose or goal, they are more inclined to collaborate and overcome obstacles. Their focus shifts from individual gratification to collective fulfillment.

4. Legacy and Impact:
- Understanding that a marriage can be the starting point of a legacy or a significant impact on society can transform the way couples approach their relationship.

The Transformative Power of Marital Purpose

The concept of a marital purpose extends beyond a mere understanding of compatibility or shared interests. It's about recognizing and committing to a higher collective goal, something that shapes every aspect of the marriage. This chapter explores the profound benefits of having a clear marital purpose. In the sacred covenant of marriage, profound truth is found - the existence of a clear and shared purpose can work wonders. Like a North Star guiding weary travelers through tumultuous seas, marital purpose steers couples through the tempests of life, keeping their love resolute and their union unbreakable.

Purpose as a Prism for Decision-Making

1. Purpose and Appreciation of the Prize:
- Drawing from the wisdom of Jesus Christ's teachings on project management, understanding the purpose of marriage is akin to understanding the cost of building a tower. It's about recognizing the investment needed – emotionally, spiritually, and practically – to achieve the desired outcome.

Take, for example, a couple whose purpose is to model and promote global peace. To embody this lofty mission, both partners must cultivate the capacity for open dialogue about their individual challenges, acknowledging their weaknesses and actively transforming them into strengths. They must also nurture the maturity to forgive and stand united against all odds, nurturing mutual respect to serve the best interests of all.

As a consultant or coach to such a couple, my role would be to craft activities that would encourage a culture of open communication, where grievances are addressed, and progress is measured at each milestone in their marital journey.

2. Purpose in Crafting a Clear Plan:

- Without a clearly articulated purpose, marital plans can become aimless, driven by individual desires rather than a unified vision.

Effective marital plans must flow from a shared vision of the desired outcome. I vividly remember Mr. and Mrs. Oluwole, a couple I interviewed after 48 years of wedded bliss. Their meticulously crafted marital plan stood as evidence of their enduring love. Each goal they set together became a reality because, over the years, their friendship had blossomed into a bond that surpassed words. They spent most of my time with them playfully bantering, demonstrating the power of shared purpose in marital planning.

3. Eliminating Distractions and Focusing on Needs:

- A clear marital purpose helps in filtering out influences and activities that don't align with the couple's goals. Just as one needs the right jacket for specific weather conditions, in marriage, choosing friends, activities, and even lifestyle choices that align with the marital purpose is crucial. This alignment ensures that the couple is not led astray by external factors that do not contribute to their shared vision.

Reflections from Personal Experiences

My experience in Winnipeg, where I faced unexpectedly harsh weather, serves as a metaphor for the importance of preparedness in marriage. I donned a jacket suitable for milder climes. Stepping out of the airport into the biting cold, I swiftly realized the mismatch between my attire and the environment.

Just as not every jacket suits every weather, not every friend or activity aligns with a couple's purpose.

Just as the right jacket is essential for the right climate, in marriage, the right influences, friends, and actions are crucial for achieving the marital purpose. Couples must be discerning in their choices, ensuring that their environment and associations contribute positively to their shared vision.

When couples are uncertain about their purpose, they risk self-sabotage by welcoming influences that diverge from their intended course. In such cases, friendships may be forged with those who thrive on gossip or negative energy, sowing seeds of discord within the marriage. To maintain the harmony and energy conducive to their purpose, couples must exercise discernment in their associations and engage in activities that resonate with their shared vision.
The essence of marital purpose lies not merely in its formulation but in its unwavering pursuit. It serves as the cornerstone of enduring love, a guiding light through the darkest nights, and a shield against the storms of distraction. In the quest for marital bliss, may couples worldwide find the clarity and resolve to uncover and fulfill their unique purpose, fostering love, understanding, and harmony that transcends the boundaries of time and place.

The Role of Purpose in Marital Success

Purpose plays a crucial role in a blissful marital experience and some of these roles include:
- **Guidance:** A clear purpose acts as a compass, guiding couples in making decisions that align with their shared goals.
- **Resilience:** It provides strength to withstand challenges, as the couple understands the higher goal they are working towards.
- **Focus:** Purpose helps couples to stay focused on what truly matters, avoiding distractions that can derail their relationship.
- **Unity:** It fosters a deeper sense of unity and partnership, as both individuals work towards a common goal.

- **Growth:** Finally, a shared purpose encourages personal and mutual growth, as each partner supports the other in achieving their collective aspirations.

Purpose Is Power

The concept of purpose in a marriage acts as a guiding light, a source of power that illuminates the path couples should tread together.

Indeed, the essence of a successful partnership lies not in attempting to do everything together but rather in the concerted effort to accomplish what is essential for realizing shared goals.

Purpose, in this context, becomes the compass that helps couples efficiently allocate their energy and maintain unwavering focus.

Through my interviews with couples from diverse backgrounds and experiences, a common thread emerges - the power of saying no to seemingly attractive opportunities in favor of what aligns with their unique purpose. It's a principle deeply ingrained in their journeys to marital success. At times, turning down enticing prospects might appear as a missed opportunity, but these couples recognized the value of preserving their energy and attention for what truly mattered.

In the face of life's myriad distractions and demands, purpose serves as a guiding force, helping couples distinguish between what's merely appealing and what's genuinely vital to their vision. It empowers them to make decisions that are in harmony with their collective goals, ensuring that they remain on course toward the fulfillment of their shared dreams.

This ability to discern, prioritize, and channel their energies toward their purpose not only strengthens their bond but also enables them to achieve remarkable results, proving that it's not about doing everything together but about doing the right things together. In the pursuit of marital success, couples worldwide can draw inspiration from these valuable insights and harness the power of purpose to chart a path of focus, unity, and commitment.

Harnessing The Power Of Purpose

1. Selective Focus for Greater Impact:

In the journey of marriage, not all opportunities are in alignment with your shared purpose. The couples I interviewed often spoke about the difficult yet crucial decisions they made to decline seemingly beneficial opportunities that didn't align with their marital goals. This selective focus is a testament to their understanding of preserving the power of purpose in their marriage.

2. A Lesson in Prioritization:

Mr. Jones's story exemplifies the importance of prioritizing one's relationship, especially during its formative years. His decision to decline a transfer that would have separated him from his wife in the early stages of their marriage reflects a profound understanding of the significance of building and nurturing their bond. The initial years of marriage are often a critical period where couples lay the foundation for a strong and lasting partnership. It's a time for getting to know each other on a deeper level, learning to navigate challenges together, and creating shared memories. Being physically apart during this phase can indeed pose challenges to the process of bonding and understanding one another.

His story serves as a reminder that while career and personal goals are essential, the relationships we cherish require deliberate attention and nurturing. By making thoughtful choices that prioritize the well-being of their marriage, couples can lay a solid foundation for a partnership that stands the test of time. His story teaches us that sometimes, the best decision is to prioritize the relationship over short-term benefits, trusting that better opportunities will arise when both partners are ready.

3. The Enduring Strength of a Purpose-Driven Marriage:

A marriage grounded in purpose is equipped to withstand the tests of time, truth, and trials. It becomes a model for others, exemplifying how focusing on a shared goal can lead to long-lasting harmony and fulfillment.

Let's reflect together on the following quiz:

- Why did you marry your spouse?
- Why did you accept his proposal?
- Why am I in this relationship?
- Why are you a wife/husband?

These questions are not mere inquiries; they are probes into the heart of your marital commitment. They challenge you to revisit and reaffirm the core reasons for your union.
Here are a couple of benefits that come with having a clear marital purpose:

- **Purpose as a Filter:** It helps in filtering out distractions, enabling couples to focus on what's essential for their growth and unity.
- **Purpose as a Bonding Agent:** Shared purpose strengthens the marital bond, fostering deeper understanding and collaboration.
- **Purpose as a Source of Resilience:** It equips couples to face challenges with a united front, knowing that every obstacle is an opportunity to strengthen their bond.
- **Purpose as a Legacy Builder:** A purpose-driven marriage sets a precedent, creating a legacy that extends beyond the couple to impact future generations.

I am sure some of you are seeking steps to creating a shared marital purpose. Here are basic tips for crafting a compelling purpose that can serve the best interest of your marriage.

Crafting a Shared Purpose

1. Identifying Individual Whys:

- The first step is for each partner to understand their own purpose. What drives you? What are your passions and deepest desires? This self-awareness is crucial before you can align your purposes as a couple.

2. Creating a Shared Vision:

- Once you understand your individual purposes, the next step is to weave them into a shared vision. This vision should be a reflection of both your purposes and should guide the trajectory of your relationship.

3. Living Your Purpose:

- A shared purpose isn't just for contemplation; it's for action. It's about making choices that align with this purpose, whether in your careers, how you raise your children, or how you contribute to your community.

4. Navigating Challenges Together:

- Challenges and obstacles are inevitable, but when you share a big WHY, these become opportunities to strengthen your bond and reaffirm your commitment to your shared goals.

Reflection Questions:

1. What is the overarching purpose of your marriage, and how does it guide your daily decisions and plans?

2. How do you ensure that your marital plans align with your shared purpose?

3. Reflect on your current friendships and activities. Do they support or hinder your marital purpose?

4. Consider a challenge in your marriage. How can your shared purpose help you navigate and overcome it?

5. In what ways can you and your partner strengthen your commitment to your shared marital purpose?

PRACTICE EMPATHY AND UNDERSTANDING

> *Seek to understand your partner's perspective, even when you disagree. Empathy fosters compassion and strengthens your connection.*

CHAPTER 6

The Standing Under Habit

In the summer of 2022, I embarked on a long flight from Dallas to Lagos, Nigeria. My destination was Lagos State, where I was tasked with training marriage registrars on implementing a new curriculum for couples preparing to wed. This journey was one I had eagerly anticipated, primarily due to my concerns about the inadequate preparation of many couples before they embark on the lifelong journey of marriage. This lack of preparation has unfortunately contributed to a disturbingly high number of cases of domestic violence, some of which have even resulted in tragic outcomes.

I am sure some of you are seeking steps to creating a shared marital purpose. Here are basic tips for crafting a compelling purpose that can serve the best interest of your marriage.

Crafting a Shared Purpose

1. Identifying Individual Whys:
- The first step is for each partner to understand their own purpose. What drives you? What are your passions and deepest desires? This self-awareness is crucial before you can align your purposes as a couple.

2. Creating a Shared Vision:
- Once you understand your individual purposes, the next step is to weave them into a shared vision. This vision should be a reflection of both your purposes and should guide the trajectory of your relationship.

3. Living Your Purpose:
- A shared purpose isn't just for contemplation; it's for action. It's about making choices that align with this purpose, whether in your careers, how you raise your children, or how you contribute to your community.

4. Navigating Challenges Together:
- Challenges and obstacles are inevitable, but when you share a big WHY, these become opportunities to strengthen your bond and reaffirm your commitment to your shared goals.

Reflection Questions:

1. What is the overarching purpose of your marriage, and how does it guide your daily decisions and plans?

2. How do you ensure that your marital plans align with your shared purpose?

...Who Is Your Spouse?

It's astonishing how often couples remain blissfully unaware of their partner's true selves. They overlook the importance of discovering who their significant other has become, shaped by various influencers such as upbringing, cultural background, and past emotional experiences. Consequently, the best version of ourselves, at our very best, is often someone else's ideal.

In my two decades of working with couples, I've consistently observed how couples' preconceived notions of an ideal spouse differ dramatically from the reality they encounter. What's more, they often cling to the hope of molding their partner into this ideal, only to discover the immense challenge this poses. Many individuals we label as "difficult" did not acquire these traits in marriage; rather, they brought them into the union. Unfortunately, some partners enter marriage with the misguided belief that they possess the power to transform their significant other into their dream spouse. This misconception can lead to disillusionment and conflict.

There are several critical areas that couples must explore in their quest to better understand one another, and I will delve into three of them:

1. Personality Types: Understanding each other's personality traits and how they influence behavior is crucial. Embracing the uniqueness of your partner's personality can pave the way for a more harmonious relationship.

2. Communication Styles: Recognizing and adapting to each other's communication styles is essential for effective and empathetic dialogue. What may be perceived as criticism could be a different style of expression.

3. Love Languages: Discovering each other's love languages—the ways in which you both give and receive love—can significantly enhance emotional intimacy. It's not just about saying "I love you" but expressing love in ways that resonate with your partner.

By exploring these areas with a genuine desire to comprehend your partner's perspective and accepting them, even with their imperfections, you can bridge the gap between your idealized notion of a spouse and the reality of the person you married.

In the realm of marriage and relationships, understanding the intricate languages of love and the nuances of individual temperaments is paramount. These elements can profoundly impact the quality and longevity of a partnership. Let's delve into these essential aspects of successful unions.

1. Understand and Accept Their Love Codes

In his widely acclaimed book, "The 5 Love Languages," Dr. Gary Chapman illuminates how people express and receive love in distinct ways. These five love languages have become the foundation of countless discussions on the dynamics of love in relationships. Yet, during one of my teaching sessions in the ancient city of Benin, Nigeria, I was struck by the revelation that not as many people are familiar with this concept as one might assume.

Dr. Chapman identifies five primary ways through which individuals typically convey love and feel loved. Couples must uncover and embrace each other's love languages, as neglecting this aspect can lead to emotional disconnection. These love languages are:

- **Words of Affirmation:** Some people thrive on verbal expressions of love and affirmation. They feel most loved when they receive words of praise, encouragement, and appreciation.

- **Physical Touch:** For others, physical touch is the primary language of love. Simple gestures like hugs, kisses, and cuddling carry profound meaning for them.

- **Acts of Service:** Some individuals interpret love through actsof service. They appreciate when their partner takes the initiative to help them, whether it's with household chores or other tasks.

- Quality Time: Quality time is the love language of those who value spending undivided attention with their partner. They feel cherished when their loved one dedicates time solely to them.

- **Gifts:** For some, gifts are tangible expressions of love. These individuals feel deeply loved when they receive thoughtful gifts, regardless of their monetary value. I've encountered situations where infidelity crept into marriages due to the neglect of these love languages. When one spouse feels deprived of their primary love language, they might seek solace in the arms of someone who fluently speaks their emotional dialect. It's crucial to understand and respect your partner's love language to nurture a fulfilling relationship.

While these concepts offer valuable insights into how individuals give and receive love and the intricacies of their personalities they should never be used as excuses for justifying negative behavior.

Understanding love languages and temperaments should enhance empathy and communication, not serve as a loophole for harmful actions or manipulation. Couples need to recognize that they remain responsible for their behavior and its consequences, irrespective of their love language or temperament.

Furthermore, embracing these concepts should not make couples overly vulnerable or expose them to harm. Instead, it should provide a framework for deeper understanding and connection. Healthy relationships are built on mutual respect, trust, and support, and understanding love languages and temperaments can contribute to these foundations.

Ultimately, the goal is to create an environment of love, understanding, and acceptance within the relationship, where both partners can thrive emotionally and personally while respecting each other's boundaries and individuality.

2. Understand and Accept Them for Who They Are (Temperaments)

The adage "treat others as you want to be treated" is a timeless principle often attributed to the Golden Rule. However, while it promotes empathy, it falls short when we consider that individuals are unique and multifaceted. Enter the Platinum Rule, popularized by Dr. Tony Alessandra, which advocates treating people as they want to be treated.

Our temperaments, a complex interplay of nature and nurture, significantly shape our personalities and interactions. In this book, I choose to explore temperaments through a prism I developed in 2007, likening people to various types of automobiles. These temperaments include:

- **Intimidating Hummers:** These natural leaders exhibit a low attention span and impatience for delays. Winning is their goal, and they may not yield easily in an argument. They prioritize work over relationships, often viewing the latter as a means to accomplish their projects.

- **Creative Convertibles:** Loved by many for their humor and magnetic personalities, these individuals are flashy and charismatic. They enjoy communicating and may have a penchant for exaggeration.

- **Dependable Trucks:** Characterized by their slow and steady decision-making style, dependable trucks excel in diplomacy. They are reliable but can struggle when confronted with impatience and hostility, as they are emotionally fragile.

- **Systematic Fords:** Perfectionists by nature, systematic Fords strive for a utopian world. They may find it challenging to forgive and harbor grudges, but their analytical skills are unparalleled. While most individuals possess a blend of these temperaments, recognizing their dominant and complementary traits is key. In doing so, couples can foster a profound acceptance of each other's personalities and maximize the benefits of their unique temperaments—whether it's leadership, fun, diplomacy, or perfectionism.

Understanding love languages and temperaments is a pivotal step toward harmonious and fulfilling relationships. It allows couples to navigate the intricate paths of human connection with empathy, grace, and authenticity.

It is important for couples to;

- **Communicate:** Regularly discuss each other's primary love languages and how to better fulfill them.

- **Empathize:** Put oneself in the partner's shoes to understand their temperamental responses and needs.

- **Adapt:** Be willing to adjust one's own behavior to better align with the partner's love language and temperament.

- **Celebrate Differences:** View differences not as obstacles but as opportunities for growth and deeper understanding.

Your perspective on relationships and marriage, emphasizing compatibility in terms of shared beliefs, temperaments, and worldviews, makes a lot of sense. While the idea that "opposites attract" is a common saying, it doesn't always translate into successful and harmonious long-term relationships.

Compatibility in key areas such as values, life goals, communication styles, and interests can be fundamental for a relationship to thrive. Couples who share common ground in these areas often find it easier to relate to each other, make decisions together, and navigate challenges as a team.
That said, it's also essential to acknowledge that there can be a balance between shared similarities and healthy differences in a relationship. While too many differences can lead to conflicts and misunderstandings, some level of complementarity can also be enriching. For example, one partner's strengths might compensate for the other's weaknesses, creating a more balanced partnership.

Ultimately, what's most important is open and effective communication within the relationship. This allows partners to understand each other's needs and preferences, make compromises when necessary, and continuously work together to build a strong and fulfilling connection.

So, while marrying someone who shares your fundamental values and interests can provide a solid foundation for a successful relationship, it's also important to maintain sense of balance and flexibility to accommodate some healthy differences that can enhance the partnership.

Opposite Attracts ➤   **Kind connects ➤**

Work   **Grace**

You talk too much	**I want to talk**	Bring it on & let's chat
I am not in the mood	**I want to have sex**	Anytime, anywhere, anyhow
It is better we maintain statusquo	**I want to take this risk**	What is the worst that can happen?
You want to turn me into someone and something else	**I want us to become more creative**	I want to explore and don't mind trying new stuff
My way is the better way	**What is the best for the children**	Let's figure out the best way and embrace it out together
I don't like crowd vs bring it on	I want to go party with friends or stay alone	I just want to be where you are

Find your kind or melt into your kind

It's interesting to see among the couples I have worked with and surveyed, similarities played a significant role in their relationships, even if they didn't consciously plan it that way. The desire to marry someone who can also be a friend and playmate is indeed a crucial factor for many successful marriages. Having a strong foundation of friendship can contribute to a deeper connection and understanding between partners. When you marry someone who not only shares your values and interests but also enjoys spending time with you as a friend, it can create a more fulfilling and enjoyable relationship.

Friendship in a marriage often involves qualities like trust, mutual respect, communication, and a willingness to support ach other's personal growth and happiness. These qualities can help couples navigate the ups and downs of life together, making the journey more pleasant and resilient. While compatibility in values and interests is essential, it's the bond of friendship that can make a marriage feel more like a partnership where both individuals genuinely enjoy each other's company and can face life's challenges together as a team.

3. Understand their worldviews and their make-up

We are all products of our past experiences, environments, and influences. In our earlier description of marriage, we portrayed it as the beautiful union of two individuals, hailing from distinct backgrounds (akin to two nations or families), intending to forge a new nation. This new union, we believe, should strive to enhance the well-being of all involved while creating a culture that brings solace and unity to our world.

When we navigate the landscape of domestic violence cases, we often employ a culture compatibility test. This test consistently unveils the clash of beliefs that tends to plague troubled couples. These conflicts frequently arise from their upbringing, surroundings, and significant emotional encounters.

It's crucial to recognize that those we label as *"problematic"* spouses are often just acting out the roles they've been scripted into. Instead of passing judgment, our endeavor should be to understand the web of influences that have shaped them. Through understanding and empathy, we can discover more effective ways to influence and guide them toward a more empowering state.

Take, for instance, the story of Charles and Adora, a couple on the brink of divorce in 2011. Their tumultuous relationship had been riddled with domestic violence. In a bid to find the root causes, I decided to conduct a culture compatibility test. Almost immediately, the test laid bare the stark incompatibility of their worldviews.

Charles firmly held certain beliefs:

- A man stands superior to a woman.
- A husband is inherently superior to his wife.
- Cooking for the family is solely a woman's duty.
- A real man does not disclose his earnings to his wife.
- A man's family members can freely enter their home whenever they please.

In stark contrast, Adora rejected these beliefs entirely. Digging deeper into the source of their beliefs led us to their upbringing and the cultural environments that had molded them. Remarkably, their two originating cultures were fundamentally at odds.

The fascinating revelation was that they had never realized the true source of their marital discord lay in their backgrounds. We all tend to navigate life based on our understanding and experiences, and they are no different. Instead of merely instructing them on how to build a good marriage, which was their genuine intention, their previous marriage counselor failed to explore how their past had influenced their present.

Their epiphany came when we embarked on a journey through their personal histories, allowing each to step into the other's shoes. After realizing that they had been unconsciously enacting scripts from their past, they began to breathe more easily. They willingly embraced a belief audit, paving the way for a shift in their beliefs.

What's truly intriguing about their worldviews is that their respective cultures had never seen anything amiss with their beliefs. While it might have been simpler for them to marry individuals who shared their beliefs, they opted for a more profound transformation. By engaging in a process of aligning their beliefs, they successfully forged new ideologies that nurtured the growth and prosperity of their marriage.

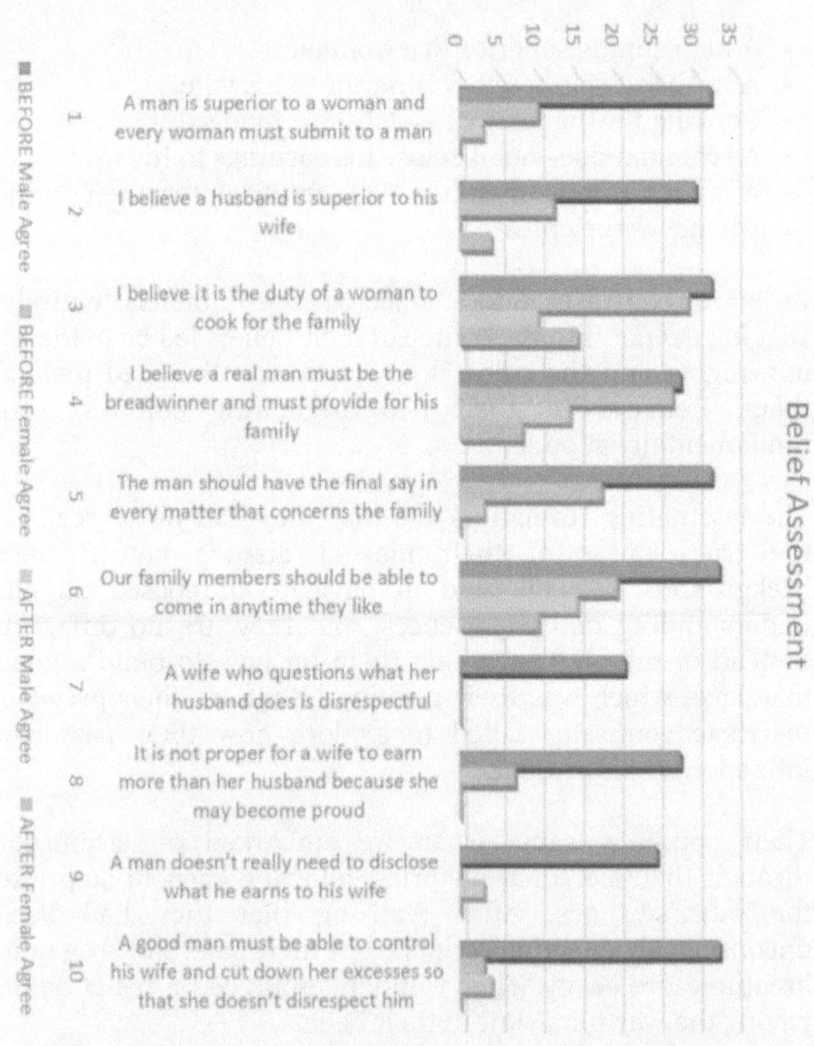

Domestic violence chart for 40 couples before and after intervention

Fostering Understanding: The Path to Empathy

When couples wholeheartedly adopt the practice of understanding, they embark on a journey of discovery. This journey involves the willingness to delve deep into the layers of behavior, searching diligently until they reach the very roots of it all. What they discover on this quest is not only expanded awareness but also a profound shift – from passing judgment to embracing empathy.

In this sacred journey of comprehension, they learn the art of stooping, not in a demeaning way, but as an act of profound humility. This gesture of humility enables them to better decipher the motivations behind each other's actions and responses. It's akin to peeling away the layers of an onion, revealing the essence within.

With each layer uncovered, they inch closer to the truth. They engage in root cause analysis, determined to unearth the underlying reasons for their behaviors and reactions. As they dig deeper, they uncover the web of influences that have shaped their thoughts, beliefs, and perspectives.

This relentless pursuit of understanding expands their awareness. It shines a light on the complexities of human nature, laying bare the vulnerabilities, fears, and insecurities that often hide beneath the surface. In the glow of this newfound awareness, judgment loses its grip.

Instead of condemning or criticizing, they find themselves embracing empathy. They recognize that every action, no matter how baffling or hurtful it may seem, has a story behind it. They begin to understand that their partner, too, is a product of their past, a canvas painted with the brushstrokes of their unique life experiences.

Empathy becomes the bridge that connects their hearts. It's the profound realization that they are not adversaries but allies in the beautiful, albeit challenging, journey of life.

They extend a hand of understanding, offering solace and support rather than condemnation.

In this atmosphere of empathy, they begin to heal. They heal not only as individuals but as a united front, a couple bound by the ties of understanding and compassion. With judgment cast aside, they find the space to communicate openly, honestly, and without fear.

Understanding becomes the cornerstone of their relationship. It fosters a deep connection, a sense of being truly seen and heard. It paves the way for growth, transformation, and the co-creation of a love that is both profound and enduring.

In the end, they discover that understanding is not merely a practice but a profound art. An art that transforms their relationship into a masterpiece, painted with the vibrant colors of empathy and love.

Reflection Questions:

1. How well do you understand and actively use your partner's love language in your daily interactions?

2. Are there aspects of your partner's temperament that you find challenging? How can you better understand and accommodate these traits?

3. In what ways can you show appreciation for your partner's unique personality and love language?

4. How do your love language and temperament complement or contrast with your partner's, and how does this affect your relationship?

5. What steps can you take to further enhance your understanding and application of your partner's love language and temperament?

CHAPTER 7

The Marital Fitness Habit

"PROFESSIONALS DO DAILY WHAT AMATEURS DO OCCASIONALLY" – GRAY PLAYER

In the spring of 2022, I found myself at the School of Contemporary African Studies at Wilfrid Laurier University in Waterloo, Canada. The trip was uneventful until I noticed something remarkable in the immigration line - a couple deeply in love. As I made my way to the immigration desk, I couldn't help but observe their affectionate display. The gentleman was not only carrying his hand luggage but also what seemed to be his beloved's. It was evident that this lady felt secure and cherished in his arms.

I have a penchant for giving compliments, and this enchanting sight was too captivating to go unnoticed. I approached the couple and praised the beautiful chemistry they shared. Their faces lit up with gratitude as they acknowledged my words. Just as I was about to move away, the lady, her smile radiant, leaned in and whispered, *"He just popped the question, and I said yes."*

This encounter left me pondering what their love would be like in two decades. While I may not have all the answers, I've gathered enough data to know that many women we've surveyed share a common sentiment - some men seem to be mere actors before marriage, going to great lengths to win their hearts, only to abandon those very actions that initially won them over.

It's not uncommon to see men sending flowers, preparing meals, and engaging in all sorts of romantic gestures during courtship, only to become complacent in marriage, neglecting the very things that influenced their partner's decision to wed.

In one of my interviews with an octogenarian couple, I recall the wise words of the wife who shared the secret to their long and happy marriage: *"Continue to do the very things that made her say Yes! I do."*

While many argue that marriage dynamics differ from premarital romance, I firmly believe that we will always find time for what truly matters to us.

In the summer of 2017, I had the opportunity to work with a celebrity who had gone through two divorces and was on the brink of giving up on love. I was the resident coach on the show and decided to delve into the similarities between her decision-making processes in accepting marriage proposals from both ex-husbands. What she revealed was shocking to everyone - the patterns were almost identical, yet she hadn't recognized them because she was convinced both relationships were genuine.

In previous chapters, we emphasized the importance of family governance systems, including family vision, values, and DNA creed. After creating these foundational elements, the next step involves crafting routines and rituals that the family must consistently engage in to bring the vision to life, as a vision without rituals is merely an idea on paper. These routines and rituals can be likened to the gym sessions that transform your body into the desired shape, promoting overall wellness.

Consider world heavyweight champion Anthony Joshua's surprising loss to underdog Andy Ruiz in 2019. It was an unexpected defeat because everyone anticipated a straightforward victory. However, Joshua triggered a rematch clause in the contract. Before the rematch, Ruiz's physical shape had deteriorated even further, and unsurprisingly, he was defeated by Joshua, who reclaimed his title.

High-level athletes like Cristiano Ronaldo have one thing in common - a steadfast commitment to their routines and rituals. Their dedication to these habits is the key to their enduring success.

In my human engineering programming course, I define routines and rituals as:

- The guaranteed path to achieving the desired results.
- The prophecy that guides you to greatness.
- The practical aspect of prayers that brings forth answers.
- The habits you master, which in turn master you.
- Your protocol for either imprisonment or a palace
- determines your ultimate destination.

Just as there is a protocol for physical fitness, there is a similar one for marital fitness. The outcomes you desire should dictate the routines you adopt.

Marital fitness consists of the actions you must consistently take and those you must avoid to create a harmonious and fulfilling marriage. It's about cultivating the habits that lead to lasting marital wellness.

To identify the right routines that can enhance marital wellness, it's essential to answer some key questions:

1. What is our marital vision? – Both partners should have a clear understanding of their shared goals and where they want their lives together to lead.

2. What has sustained our marriage or what did we cherish most before getting married? – Reflect on the elements that have been the bedrock of your relationship or what initially drew you together. These can provide insights into what needs to be preserved to maintain marital wellness. If certain disciplines or behaviors were crucial in reaching your current state, consider if they are still applicable or if higher levels of dedication are necessary to sustain your connection.

3. What triggers negative emotions in my spouse? – Identify the actions or behaviors that upset your partner. Understanding these triggers allows you to avoid them and take proactive steps to prevent unnecessary conflicts.

4. What regular activities should we incorporate into our routine to nurture our relationship? – Establish a list of weekly or monthly activities that you both commit to consistently. These activities should contribute to the health and growth of your relationship. Whether they are daily check-ins, weekly date nights, or monthly getaways, regular

interaction and shared experiences can strengthen your bond.

By addressing these questions and implementing the insights gained, you can build routines that promote a healthy and enduring marital connection.

Here Is A Sample Fitness Chart

NAME	THE JONES
Family vision	To create a team of loving friends who freely express their highest abilities in raising other winning families to transform our world
What did we enjoy the most before marriage	1. Friday movie night 2. Weekly romantic love notes 3. Monthly book review 4. His weekly supply of grilled peppered fish
Do you still engage in these activities together? If no at what point did you stop?	We no longer do them and we just got busy and it naturally stopped
Do you still feel as happy as you were in the relationship?	Not at all because we practically live as housemates
What do we need to stop	1. Judgements 2. Too many religious activities 3. Hanging out with friends without creating time for ourselves
What must we start that can keep us fit	<table><tr><td>ACTIVITY</td><td>DATE</td></tr><tr><td>1. Friday movie night</td><td>Every Friday</td></tr><tr><td>2. Daily spousal gratitude journal</td><td>Daily before bedtime</td></tr><tr><td>3. Monthly personality review</td><td>3rd Sunday of every month</td></tr><tr><td>4. Monthly peppered fish party</td><td>Last Friday of every month</td></tr><tr><td>5. Date night</td><td>16th of every month</td></tr></table>

In the year 2022, Manchester United, one of Britain's most storied football clubs, made a pivotal decision to hire Eric Ten Hag as their new head coach. The club had experienced a tumultuous period of experimentation with several coaches, and their glory days seemed to have faded into the past.

Upon assuming office, Eric Ten Hag, with the keen eye of a strategist, swiftly identified a critical issue that was plaguing the team – their fitness. The players were not in the physical condition required to perform at their best. Recognizing that greatness could only be achieved through relentless effort and discipline, Ten Hag embarked on a mission to restore the team's lost glory.

His first move was a radical overhaul of the players' dietary habits. He understood that nutrition played a pivotal role in transforming the team's fitness levels. One of the immediate changes he introduced was the compulsory measurement of Body Mass Index (BMI) on a weekly basis. This seemingly simple yet profound alteration was met with resistance from some players who were accustomed to indulging in their culinary desires without restraint.

The transformation didn't happen overnight. In the first two matches of the season, Manchester United faced off against supposedly weaker opponents and suffered unexpected losses. The outcome was a stark reflection of their inadequate fitness levels. Detailed analytics showed that, during those matches, they ran less than their competitors – a clear indicator of their physical shortcomings.

Eric Ten Hag's response was unyielding in its pursuit of excellence. He demanded an immediate return to the training grounds, even on what would have been a rest day. The players, along with Ten Hag himself, were put through a grueling 14-kilometer run. It was a test of their endurance, a measure of their commitment, and a declaration of their collective will to succeed.

What transpired next was nothing short of miraculous. The following match, one that everyone anticipated as a loss against their arch-rivals and one of Europe's top teams over the past three years, ended in a surprising victory for Manchester United.

This triumph marked the beginning of a remarkable streak, with the team securing victories in their next four games, including an astonishing win against the previously unbeaten Arsenal.

This sporting saga serves as a powerful metaphor for life. It underscores the undeniable connection between relentless effort, discipline, and the realization of one's highest potential. Eric Ten Hag's vision and determination breathed new life into a team that had lost its way. In much the same way, individuals and couples can draw inspiration from this tale, understanding that the path to excellence is paved with resilience, discipline, and a relentless commitment to the journey.

1. On which days must you engage in these activities? Determining what days of the week, month, or year you must engage in your marital fitness activities is not just about identifying these crucial actions; it's about dedicating time and commitment to them. I vividly recall a life-changing lesson I learned from my mentor many years ago when I found myself struggling to balance the demands of work and family, often leaving me with insufficient time for my children. His wisdom reshaped my priorities and significantly improved my life. He shared a formula that, when applied diligently, could harmonize the various aspects of life based on their importance in one's hierarchy of values.

Here's how it works, and it has the potential to be life-saving for anyone facing similar challenges:

A. Block Out Family Time: At the start of each year, schedule and firmly block out dates dedicated to your family. These are sacred times when you prioritize spending quality moments with your loved ones. Protect these dates as you would guard your most treasured possessions.

B. Prioritize Organizational Functions: Next in line are the dates reserved for your most critical organizational functions and commitments. These are occasions and tasks that contribute significantly to the growth and development of your professional endeavors. While essential, they should come after your family commitments in your calendar.

C. Allocate Time for External Events: Finally, allocate dates for external events and functions hosted by others, such as invitations to gatherings or conferences. These are important opportunities for networking and engagement beyond your immediate circles.

This formula is nothing short of life-changing because it helps you maintain a delicate balance between various aspects of your life. Too often, people become ensnared by the demands of work or external obligations, unintentionally neglecting their family and personal well-being.

2. Remember, every time you sacrifice your scheduled family fitness sessions for other engagements, you risk becoming emotionally and relationally unfit. Just as an athlete needs consistent training to maintain peak performance, your marriage requires regular nurturing and attention to thrive. Prioritizing your family, dedicating time to your relationship, and honoring your commitments to marital fitness are key to ensuring that your marriage remains strong, vibrant, and able to withstand the tests of time.

3. What obstacles may arise, and how will you overcome them? It's essential to be proactive in your approach to

anticipate potential disruptions to your marital fitness routine and have a well-thought-out plan to address them. Life is unpredictable, and challenges can emerge unexpectedly, but having a clear strategy in place can serve as your anchor during turbulent times.

Consider various scenarios and challenges that could hinder your commitment to your marital fitness activities. These obstacles might include conflicts, external pressures, or emotional turmoil that could disrupt your routine. By identifying these potential roadblocks in advance, you're better prepared to face them head-on.

HERE'S HOW YOU CAN APPROACH THIS ASPECT OF MARITAL FITNESS:

- **Communicate these scenarios:** Together with your partner, engage in scenario planning. Discuss possible situations that could impact your fitness routine negatively. This might involve conflicts, work-related stress, health issues, or family emergencies. Openly communicate about these scenarios, and ensure you both have a mutual understanding of how to handle them.

- **Clear Communication:** Establish a communication plan for when obstacles arise. Agree on how you'll discuss these challenges, ensuring that your discussions are constructive and solution-focused rather than leading to further discord. Communication is a powerful tool for resolving issues and maintaining emotional connection.

- **Alternative Strategies:** Develop alternative strategies for staying on track with your marital fitness routine during challenging times. These strategies might involve modifying your activities, adjusting schedules, or finding new ways to support each other emotionally. Flexibility is key in adapting to unforeseen circumstances.

- **Seeking Support:** Recognize when external support is needed. Whether it's seeking guidance from a therapist or counselor, turning to friends and family for advice, or joining support groups, there are resources available to help navigate difficult times. Be open to seeking assistance when necessary, as it can strengthen your relationship.

- **Record Your Solutions:** Document your agreed-upon solutions and strategies for overcoming obstacles. Having a written record can serve as a reference point during challenging moments and prevent miscommunication or misunderstandings.

- **Regular Review:** Periodically revisit your obstacle mitigation plan. Life circumstances change, and what works during one phase of your marriage might need adjustments later on. Regularly reviewing and updating your plan ensures it remains effective and relevant.

By proactively addressing potential obstacles and developing a solid plan to overcome them, you and your partner can strengthen your bond and maintain your commitment to marital fitness. Remember that challenges are a natural part of any relationship, and how you face them together can define the resilience and longevity of your marriage.

In marital fitness, script your own story of enduring love, where each step leads to a closer, more intimate embrace. Just as athletes cherish their routines, cherish the rituals that keep your love strong.

Reflection Questions

1. What are the most significant insights or takeaways from the discussion on marital fitness and routine?

2. How can you apply the concept of routine and rituals to improve your own marital wellness?

3. Reflect on the importance of clear communication and mutual understanding in maintaining a healthy marriage. How can you enhance these aspects in your relationship?

4. Consider the analogy between physical fitness and marital fitness. What parallels do you see, and how can these insights guide your actions in maintaining a strong marriage?

5. Think about the obstacles and challenges that can arise in a marriage. How can proactive planning and open communication help you overcome these hurdles?

6. What are the routines or rituals that you believe are essential for your marital fitness? How do these activities contribute to the well-being of your relationship?

7. Reflect on the role of priorities in your life. Are there adjustments you need to make to ensure that your family and marriage receive the attention they deserve?

8.How do you view the long-term goals and vision of your marriage? What steps can you take to align your beliefs and actions with this vision?

9. Consider the importance of flexibility and adaptation in maintaining a healthy marriage. How can you and your partner stay resilient in the face of changing circumstances?

10. Reflect on the stories and examples shared in this piece, such as Manchester United's fitness transformation. What lessons can you draw from these narratives to improve your relationship?

FORGIVE
AND LET GO

Holding onto resentment only poisons the relationship. Learn to forgive each other's mistakes and let go of past hurts, focusing instead on building a brighter future together.

CHAPTER 8

The Power of Team Spirit

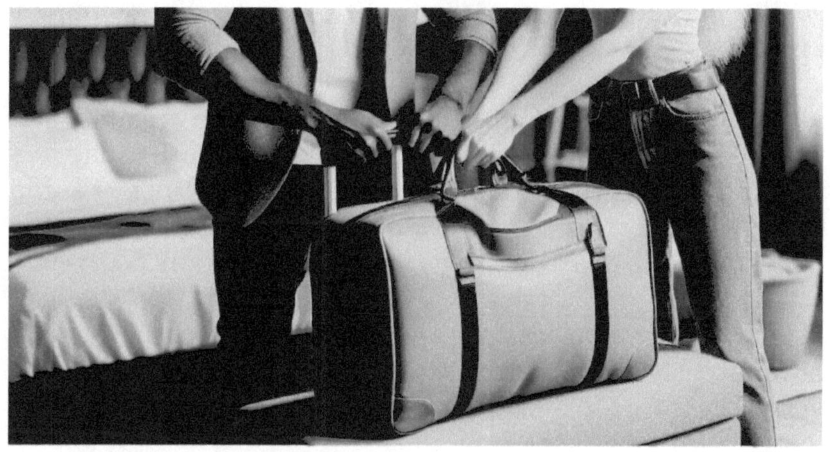

In football history, some moments are beyond the boundaries of the sport, moments that become emblematic of resilience, unity, and the sheer power of the human spirit. One such moment unfolded in the scorching heat of Saudi Arabia in 1989 during the U-20 FIFA World Youth Championship. It was a quarter-final clash between Nigeria and the formidable USSR, and the world was about to witness a spectacle of epic proportions.

As an impressionable 11-year-old, I remember that day vividly. Nigeria, a nation yearning for good news amidst political turbulence, had pinned its hopes on this tournament. My father, an Anglican Priest of strict demeanor, was one of countless

Nigerians seeking solace in the beautiful game. When a football match kicked off, my dad's stern countenance would often soften, and the promise of free drinks only sweetened the deal.

The match began with a thunderous pace, but to our dismay, the USSR swiftly seized a 2-goal lead. The Nigerian team's shoulders slumped in self-blame, the weight of the deficit crushing their spirits. In a desperate bid to change the tide, the coaching staff substituted Angus Ikeji, the beleaguered goalkeeper, for Emeka Amadi. Yet, the USSR, seemingly unstoppable, notched two more goals.

My father's disappointment was palpable, and I feared that my dream of sharing a bottle of coke with him that day was slipping away. But then, a remarkable transformation occurred. In a moment that would go down in history as the *"Dammam Miracle,"* the Nigerian U-20 team rallied.

As the fourth goal was scored against us, the USSR team began to play to the gallery, overconfident in their impending victory.

But what was truly astonishing was the newfound cohesion within the Nigerian team. They started playing as a unit, with an urgency that had been missing. It was as if they'd embraced the adage, *"He that is down needs fear no fall."*

With 30 minutes left on the clock, the unthinkable began to take shape. The Nigerian team fought for their lives. Christopher Ohenhen, a free-kick specialist, displayed his prowess, netting two goals. And with two more goals before the final whistle, we achieved the impossible—equalizing from a 4-goal deficit. My dad, witnessing this astonishing turnaround, rushed back home as if he'd seen a miracle.

The match entered extra time and, ultimately, a nerve-wracking penalty shootout. Nigeria emerged triumphant, etching their names in the annals of football history. They became the first team to mount a comeback from a four-goal deficit, equalize, and then clinch victory in a World Cup game at any level.

Reflecting on that historic match, football analysts pointed to the unbreakable team spirit of the Nigerian squad. It was their unity, their belief in one another, that paved the way for such a miraculous turnaround.

This tale from the world of football is a testament to the profound impact of team spirit—a force capable of beating insurmountable odds and igniting the human potential for greatness. It reminds us that as we navigate the complex game of life, fostering unity, resilience, and belief in our shared goals can lead to miracles of our own making.

Is Your Marital Team Spirit Intact?

Marriage, much like a football team competing in a league, embarks on a journey year after year with a clear agenda: to build a peaceful and harmonious world together. Teams, whether in sports or marriage, understand that the quality of their players, their ability to blend into the team, and the superior tactical formations are key to winning matches. In the world of marriage, ignorance of your team's playing pattern can spell failure, just as not understanding your partner's tactics and how to navigate them can lead to marital breakdown.

I've consistently emphasized that star players don't win games; it takes an entire team to secure victory. You'll never see a scoreline that looks like

This is because the essence of a team is collaboration. Couples, too, must see themselves as a team, working together toward their shared vision. The critical ingredient that distinguishes great teams from mediocre ones is known as TEAM SPIRIT.

Team spirit is the glue that helps couples withstand the trials of life and work harmoniously toward their common goals. It means that even when we hurt, we don't stand in the way of our purpose. We forgive because of what we must achieve together. This collective mindset keeps the marriage intact. A discovery from observing over 40 couples who went through a divorce is that the marriage often split when team spirit was broken, replaced by individualism.

Psychologist Bruce Tuckman's team formation stages— forming, storming, norming, and performing shed light on the journey of a team. However, many marriages falter between the storming and norming phases, struggling to manage conflicts and disagreements.

Today, there is no winning team in any arena that hasn't weathered storms and faced crises. Similarly, no marriage is exempt from trials. Yet, what sets apart couples who navigate these challenges successfully is their commitment to the purpose of their marriage and their resolute team spirit.

Mr. and Mrs. Grumby, married for 56 years, shared invaluable wisdom: *"Never let external factors or individual challenges interfere with your genuine feelings for each other. As long as your true feelings remain intact, you can always bounce back"*

In this digital age of whispers, marital woes echo across screens. Some turn marital strife into a spectacle for profit, seeking validation through clicks and views. Online juries now pass verdicts on unions, shaping the marital tribulations.

In this whirlwind of modernity, my counsel holds true: keep your private world away from the public glare, and invite a sage, a professional, to help decipher your riddles. Amid the tempest, it's the fire of team spirit and shared dreams that will light your path to love's triumph.

HERE ARE SOME REASONS TEAM SPIRIT IS BROKEN:

The Fractured Spirit of Love

In the arena of love's dance, there are moments when the harmonious symphony of togetherness falters, and the spirit of unity wavers. Here, within longing hearts, we uncover the reasons behind this lamentable fracture:

Sustaining Love's Resilient Spirit

Within the delicate folds of love, preservation strategies are threads of resilience, weaving strength into the union.

1. Lack of marital vision: Many of the troubled marriages we have worked with did not come across as people with a uniform vision.

2. Undefined marital formation: Every couple plays a marital formation that ideally should be agreed on before marriage unfortunately people step into marriage with a lot of assumptions such that while one person may see marriage as a team the other sees an autocratic system where the spouse is a servant and not a team mate.

3. Unresolved trauma and hurts: I sometimes facilitate couple's forums and many couples are hurting yet bottling things up. Many are on the verge of murdering their spouse yet never uttered a word until those sessions.

4. External influence: Every marriage is supposed to be like a country with sovereignty but there is often a lot of interference by people who come with stories that can upset the peace of the family. These external influences could be family, friends, or even influence from movies and pop culture.

5. Personal Filters: These are filters through which we all process reality and this often gets in the way in the way couples relate with themselves. Your filters include:

- Beliefs
- Values
- Memories
- Decisions
- Attitudes
- Languages
- Meta programs

Your filters are how we process realities and they are often a product of our upbringing, environment, and significant emotional experience. Once our filters are subjective, the screen through which we interpret starts to affect what we see. For example, a lady whose father cheated on her mum may struggle with trusting her husband even if he is a saint.

Couples must have major strategies for preserving their team spirits because your marriage stands no chance if you don't create a system that can help you preserve what you both share. I will share about 3 of them.

- Create your hurt indicators, registers, and response (HRR). This is one strategy that has helped many of my clients preserve their team spirit and it is ridiculously easy to apply that they often wonder why they never heard about it before. Imagine a dance where the heart leads and hurt is met with grace; it's a ballet of emotions, a symphony of love—the Hurt Indicators, Registers, and Response (HRR) strategy. It's the thread that stitches the hearts of lovers, the guardian of team spirit.

Society often scripts a different drama—a tale where a furrowed brow or simmering anger speaks louder than words when wounds are fresh. Couples, in moments of distress, may retreat into silence, longing for their partner to decode their inner turmoil. This unspoken agony can be a source of frustration for both.

Now, think of an alternative—a world where hurt finds expression in gentle gestures and open words. An era where hurt is acknowledged and responded to, without building walls of anger and resentment. This is the era of HRR.

HRR is a language of love—a predetermined register representing the depth of hurt and the desired response. It's the whispered script for the ballet of healing, written in the heart's ink.

Imagine that you are surrounded by friends, and your beloved performs an action that unsettles you. Instead of retreating into a stormy silence, you gaze into her eyes with a smile. In that look lies your hurt, encoded in the unspoken language you've both embraced. You ask about the king-size red wine she once served, a wine you've never shown interest in before.

In that instant, she understands red wine is the pre-determined register to capture the pains you feel. She realizes she has wounded you. But it doesn't end there. Her response is the overture to reconciliation, an act rehearsed through shared understanding. She walks to you, her touch as gentle as a breeze, and embraces you, promising an even better version of that wine.

In just ten minutes, anger dissolves, and your bond remains unbroken. What might have taken days to mend is swiftly restored, leaving onlookers unaware of the tempest that briefly passed.

Such is the magic of HRR—a bridge over troubled waters, a refuge of understanding. It may not mend deep chasms or handle irreparable wounds, but it is a beacon through the fog of everyday misunderstandings.

- Agree and implement the OPEN DAY SYSTEM(ODS).

The Open Day System (ODS)
In love, there exists a sacred space—an arena where hearts lay bare their truths, where words flow freely without fear of judgment or repercussion. It's a sanctuary known as the Open Day System (ODS), a sanctuary of the soul.

The genesis of ODS is shrouded in the mists of time. Its creation was an act of love, a response to the desire to keep the corridors of their hearts free from the cobwebs of bottled emotions. As the architects of their love story, they envisioned a day each week when the heart's whispers could find voice and thoughts could take form without fear.

My first ODS as a married man arrived like a revelation, an awakening. With trepidation, we ventured into the waters of transparency. My wife, with a gentle gaze, declared her vexation: *"You irritate me with the way your cutleries make noise and the way you rush your food."*

My heart, initially startled, listened. For in her words, I discovered not criticism but an invitation to a journey through the archives of my past. I journeyed back to the days of youth, when shared meals were contests, and finishing first was the triumph. This realization became the catalyst for transformation because I didn't know I had become unconsciously competent at winning my food contest as a way of defeating those who were coming to share my food after eating their own.

I decided to work on myself seeking her support and understanding. In just four weeks, I learned better dining manners, one where the hurried rhythm of the past no longer played. My next open day revealed a symphony of thoughtful consumption.

Open day—a chosen day of the week, is a canvas for raw expression, a stage for unfiltered voices. Here, within the In this haven, essential rules are followed:

- Anger finds no sanctuary because no one is allowed to be angry.
- Defense remains at the door because you can't be defensive.
- The spoken word carries no chains which means whatever is said can't be used against the person who said it.
- If the heart's lament touches the essence of your beloved, transformation becomes your sacred promise and you must work on effective the needed change.

Since the dawn of the ODS journey, countless couples have embraced this practice, sparing themselves the havoc of suppressed emotions. ODS stands as a sentinel against the darkness of misunderstandings, a beacon guiding them to the shores of understanding.

In the tender light of love, ODS thrives—a sanctuary where hearts find solace, a testament to their commitment to the art of listening, the poetry of communication, and the symphony of transformation.

Since we started this open-day system so many couples have prevented what could have been a devastating repercussion for bottled emotions.

Here is a testimony that was sent in by Joyce from Indianapolis.

Dear Praise,

I wanted to take a moment to express my deepest gratitude for your incredible work on your YouTube channel, especially concerning family life. Your platform truly feels like a global family life classroom, and I wanted to share how it profoundly impacted my life.

I stumbled upon one of your videos during a challenging period in my life. I was wrestling with a painful secret, and I didn't know how to handle it. It felt like I was trapped in a cycle of hurt and pretense. Your wisdom spoke to me, and I decided to dive even deeper by enrolling in one of your courses where you extensively covered the concept of the open day.

At that point, I was contemplating some dark thoughts, torn between despair and desperation. I knew my spouse was being unfaithful, but I had kept it buried inside, unable to confront the issue. The pain was eating away at me.

Then came your course, and during the open-day system discussion, something remarkable happened. My husband happened to be home with me when I was listening to this part of your course. I summoned the courage to be brutally honest with him. I confessed that I had been harboring thoughts of harming him and myself due to the immense emotional turmoil.

My husband was taken aback, understandably shocked by my revelation. But, as I continued to share my feelings and what I had discovered, something truly miraculous occurred. My confession seemed to break a dam that had been holding back our emotions. My husband, who had been unaware of the extent of my suffering, broke down in tears. It was as if a heavy burden was lifted from my chest.

At that moment, we made a significant decision. We decided to seek guidance through your coaching sessions. Praise, I want you to know that your coaching has completely transformed our family. My husband has become more accountable, addressing the underlying issues that had caused us so much pain.

Thank you for your wisdom, compassion, and the incredible family framework you shared with us. Our family has taken a new and positive turn, and we owe it all to you.

With profound gratitude,

Joyce

- **Predetermine the cost of drifting apart**

In my annual goal-setting classes, I often encounter individuals whose aspirations remain unmet. These dreams languish in the shadows, unfulfilled, for there exists no tangible consequence for their abandonment. The cost of failure, it seems, does not bear a weight substantial enough to stir their spirits. Scoring a mere forty percent feels sufficient, as someone else might step in to bridge the gap. But, let me share the story of a remarkable lady, a student in one of my classes. Within a single year, she shattered her goals, achieving the extraordinary.

The catalyst for her transformation lay in a simple yet potent act. She simulated the consequence of failing to achieve her goals as nothing less than the loss of eleven of her dearest souls. With that specter hanging over her, she was resolute in her commitment to success.

Imagine if the cost of drifting apart from your spouse meant the loss of those most precious to your heart, would divorce still hold for you?

Once the cost is defined, couples stand at a juncture. They must create a robust system to analyze and conquer any impending threat to their shared dreams. It is this strategic fortitude that safeguards the cherished team spirit, preserving the union so dear to their hearts.

End note reflection questions

1. Have you ever considered the potential consequences of drifting apart in your relationship? What do you think might be a significant enough cost to deter you from such a path?

2. Reflect on a situation in your life where a well-defined consequence or reward motivated you to take significant action. How did this experience shape your understanding of how human decisions are influenced?

3. What steps can you take with your partner to predetermine the cost of drifting apart in your relationship? How might this exercise enhance your commitment to one another?

4. Consider the concept of consequences in a relationship. How do consequences, whether positive or negative, impact the dynamics between couples? Are there any specific consequences you'd like to establish to strengthen your bond?

5. How do you envision preserving your team spirit as a couple? What strategies could you develop to safeguard your relationship against potential threats or challenges?

KEEP
ROMANCE ALIVE

Never underestimate the power of romance. Surprise each other, flirt, and keep the spark alive through small gestures of love and affection.

CHAPTER 9

The Dance of Continuous Evolution: Embracing Change in Marriage

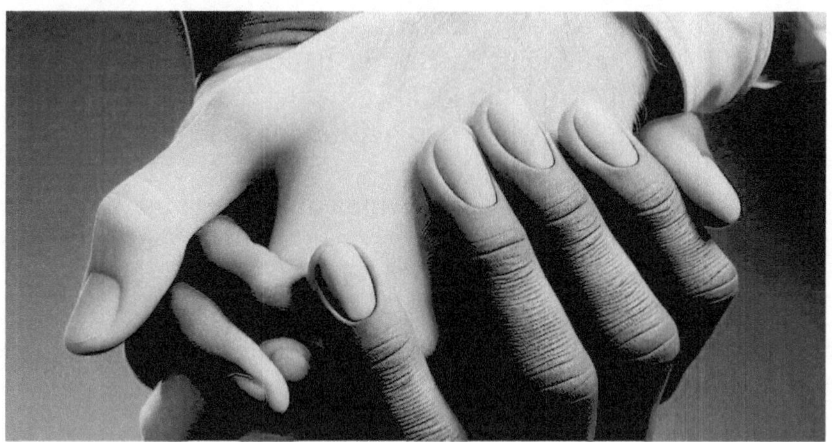

APPETITES & DESIRES WILL CHANGE AND
WE MUST UPGRADE TO MATCH THE CHANGE

In the embrace of San Diego's perpetual holiday spirit, during a family life conference in 2022, I found myself pondering the fluidity and evolution inherent in marital relationships. This city, with its endless summer vibe, mirrored the evolving nature of love and companionship that I was there to speak about.

As I stepped out of the airport, the air rich with the scent of the ocean, I found my thoughts interrupted by an insistent ring. A woman, her voice laced with the rich tones of African heritage, reached out from the brink of marital dissolution, seeking illumination. "I've received ample training to address such issues using our revolutionary psychometry tool called 'Oyela' (a term from southwestern Nigeria meaning 'Illumination'). I collected her details and sent an email to both she and her husband, inviting them to take the assessments." Employing 'Oyela', our unique tool of psychometric analysis, we went on a journey to unravel the real issues in her relationship.

Analysis painted a picture of two souls who had drifted into uncharted territories over five years. A couple, once entwined in love, now stood as strangers, their paths diverged. The catalyst? A seismic shift in the husband's career trajectory, propelling him into personal growth and development, leaving his partner anchored in a different space.

As he soared, embraced by the winds of change and corporate ascendancy, she remained, her world revolving around the hearth and home. The gap widened with each of his expeditions into self-improvement and global exposure, his tastes and perspectives evolving, leaving her ensnared in the webs of yesteryears.

In this transformation, their love became an unwitting casualty. Her once cherished simplicity now seemed a discordant note in his evolved life. Their home, once a haven, now echoed with discontent, the mundane becoming unbearable under his new lens of sophistication. Unknown to them, they had become victims of a critical habit that the most effective marriages embrace – continuous development.

This story is a testament to the perils of intellectual incompatibility – a divergence in worldviews and personal growth that can erode the foundations of even the strongest marriages. It's a stark reminder that in love, as in life, one must either evolve together or risk being torn apart by the tides of change.

People evolve; it's an undeniable fact. They say that the only constant in life is change, and I often remind people that failing to proactively lead change will leave them behind because change is inevitable.

One of the common mistakes couples make is not keeping track of their personal growth and the transformations happening in their lives.

During my research, I encountered a couple who shared a valuable practice they had adopted. They call it 'What's New.' Each week, they engage in a debriefing session where they discuss new things they've learned and how their beliefs and actions have evolved. This keeps them on the same page, ensuring their intellectual compatibility.

Intellectual incompatibility often arises when couples' worldviews no longer align with what they held when they first got married.

In marriage, we must dance to the ever-changing rhythms of life, Together, evolving, growing in unison, In this dance of continuous evolution, Lies the secret to an enduring, fulfilling love. In the romantic city of San Diego, I learned that love, like its streets basking in eternal sunlight, must evolve, grow, and adapt.

It's not just about walking together but evolving together, continuously rediscovering each other in the journey of life. In the ever-changing world of relationships, various factors can create gaps between partners, necessitating continuous adaptation and understanding.

They include:

1. The Influence of New Awareness

As we journey through life, new experiences and insights can significantly alter our perceptions and responses. This is akin to two individuals attending the same seminar but emerging with vastly different takeaways. For instance, topics like oral sex, once not discussed in older generations, are now more openly explored by contemporary couples. This shift in awareness can lead to discrepancies in comfort levels and expectations within a marriage.

As these waves of new awareness lap at the shores of our relationships, they often bring with them a shift in comfort levels and expectations. What was once a shared harbor of understanding may now feel like a sea of unfamiliarity. This evolving awareness asks us to not only acknowledge these changes but to hold them gently, to approach them with curiosity and openness.

It beckons us to engage in deeper conversations, to explore these new realms of understanding together, and to recalibrate our shared compass. This journey is not about resisting the tides of change but about learning to sail together on these new waters, finding rhythm and harmony during transformation.

2. The Impact of New Exposure

In marriage, the winds of new exposure carry with them the seeds of transformation, planting them in the fertile soils of our shared lives. Travel and exposure to different cultures can profoundly impact one's worldview.

Imagine the experience of travel, not just as a physical journey to distant lands, but as a voyage across the vast oceans of culture and perspective. For many, particularly those hailing from the developing corners of our world, this journey shows landscapes of efficiency and advancement that starkly contrast the familiar terrains of home. It is not uncommon for these travelers, especially the younger generation, to find themselves captivated by these new vista, often becoming reluctant to return to what they now perceive as the limitations of their native lands .

This phenomenon of new exposure is akin to viewing the world through a newly discovered wide-angle lens, one that broadens perspectives and alters long-held beliefs. My marital journey echoes this theme of transformation through new exposure. When my wife returned from her academic pursuits in the United Kingdom, she brought back more than just knowledge and a degree. Her time abroad had subtly reshaped her being, infusing her with new perspectives and ways of being that were unfamiliar to our life together.

This shift, though enriching, initially manifested as friction between us. It was a dance of adjustment, where each step of understanding and adaptation was crucial to rediscovering our harmony. It took us close to two years but we eventually adjusted to each other. It underscored the need for both partners in a marriage to not only recognize but also embrace the changes brought about by new exposures.

The journey of adapting to these new perspectives is not merely about acknowledgment; it's about weaving these new threads into the shared vision of marriage. It calls for conversations that bridge worlds, for empathy that reaches across new divides, and for a love that is flexible enough to encompass these evolving dimensions of each other.

It's about understanding that each journey, each experience outside the familiar, can add depth and color to the marital relationship. It's about learning to dance to the evolving tunes of your partner's soul, to find joy in the new shades of their personality, and to build bridges across the expanded landscapes of their world.

In the end, the impact of new exposure in marriage is about growing together, learning to thrive amidst change, and celebrating the unfolding horizons of each other's worlds.

It's a testament to the resilient and adaptive nature of love, a love that is not static, but dynamic and ever-expanding.

3. The Role of New Relationships

In marriage, new relationships often waltz into our lives, each step bringing with it the potential for profound influence. These relationships, be they mentorships or professional connections, carry with them the seeds of transformation, subtly reshaping our perspectives and values. Leadership in this context becomes a dance of influence, where the most impactful movements are often the most subtle.

Imagine a new leader arriving in an organization, an image of excellence, their ethos and standards becoming a new rhythm to which everyone begins to sway. This cultural shift in the workplace can ripple through to the home, creating dissonance if the domestic environment doesn't echo this newfound pursuit of excellence. It is here that the art of change management becomes pivotal in the symphony of family life, ensuring that the home doesn't become a discordant note but rather joins in this new melody of growth and excellence.

In my own love story, this theme of subtle influence was evident. My wife, during our dating years, had her literary preferences, which did not align with my passion for self-development literature. Recognizing her unique tastes, yet also seeing the potential for her growth in the new literary world, I crafted a strategy that was both gentle and persuasive.

In moments of shared quietude, I would ask her to read a chapter of my current book to me, creating a cozy tableau with my head resting in her lap. This was more than just a shared reading session; it was an invitation to a new world of ideas and perspectives. It was an act of subtle influence, a way to introduce her to these empowering narratives without imposing my choices upon her.

The magic of this strategy unfolded gracefully. As she lent her voice to these words of growth and wisdom, she found herself drawn into their power and allure. Soon, she began to seek out these books herself, asking for copies of whatever I was reading.

This shared journey into the world of self-development literature became a harmonious part of our relationship, often leading us to beautiful synchrony in our thoughts and responses to life's various scenarios.

In the end, the influence of new relationships in marriage is a delicate balance. It's about embracing change while respecting individuality, about guiding each other toward growth while honoring personal choices. It's a dance of subtlety and understanding, where the gentle sway of influence can lead to a harmonious and enriched union.

In the evolving journey of life and marriage, there are facets of our being that are like leaves in the wind, ever-changing and reshaping with the passing seasons.

They include:

1. The Malleability of Beliefs

Consider the nature of beliefs: they are not immutable truths etched in stone but rather are akin to colors with which we paint our understanding of the world. As children, our beliefs are simple yet vivid – a toy snake can embody both the thrill of danger and the safety of play. As we grow, these beliefs evolve, shedding their former skins, much like how we outgrow the fears and fantasies of childhood.

This evolution of belief is especially poignant as we ascend the rungs of our careers and open our eyes to new insights and understandings. The corporate ladder, for instance, is more than just a climb of professional achievement; it's a journey that often requires a reconfiguration of our beliefs and perspectives.

The Importance of Synchronizing Beliefs in Marriage

In marriage, partners must move in rhythm to the music of evolving beliefs. If one partner soars in their professional or personal development, embracing new philosophies and worldviews, and the other remains anchored in the past, discordance emerges. It's akin to a duet where one dancer evolves their steps, and the other persists with the old routine. To avoid being left behind in this dance, it's crucial to remain attuned to each other's growth. Engaging in open dialogues about these changing beliefs, being receptive to new ideas, and being willing to let go of outdated notions are steps toward maintaining harmony.

Bruce Lee's wisdom encapsulates this concept perfectly: "The more aware you become, the more you shed from day to day what you have learned so that your mind is always fresh and uncontaminated by previous conditioning." It's a reminder that true wisdom lies in the ability to continually learn and unlearn, to keep our minds supple and open to the new breezes of change.

As partners in life's journey, embracing this fluidity of beliefs is not just about personal growth; it's about growing together. It's about recognizing that the beliefs we hold today might not serve us tomorrow and that our shared path is enriched by this constant process of evolving and adapting our understandings. In the end, the changing nature of our beliefs offers an opportunity for deeper connection and synchronicity in marriage. It's about creating a dance where both partners are continually learning, unlearning, and relearning together, keeping their steps beautifully aligned with the rhythm of life's ever-changing melody.

2. The Evolution of Appetite

In the ballet of life and marriage, 'appetite' is a fluid and ever evolving entity, changing its rhythm and pace as the years unfold. Just as a river's course alters with the landscape, so too do our desires and cravings transform as we journey through the different seasons of our lives. Reflect upon the youthful days, when certain cravings and desires seemed all-encompassing, their fulfillment central to our happiness. These appetites, be they for the thrill of adventure, the intensity of physical passions, or the allure of material luxuries, once defined our choices and dreams. Yet, as time weaves its intricate tapestry, these once fervent desires often mellow, their edges softened by wisdom, experience, and shifting priorities.

Consider, sexual appetite for instance. In the spring of youth, it may have held a central place in our spectrum of desires. However, as we age, its intensity may wane or transform, making room for deeper, and more subtle forms of intimacy and connection. Similarly, the pursuit of luxury and material indulgences, once a driving force, may gradually yield to a quest for simplicity, contentment, and deeper, more meaningful life experiences.

Communication: The Key To Navigating Change

In the sacred union of marriage, these shifts in appetite can be sources of misunderstanding and disconnect if not navigated with care and openness. When couples fail to communicate effectively about the changes occurring within and around them, their relationship can encounter turbulent waters. It is crucial, therefore, for partners to engage in honest, open dialogues about their evolving desires and needs.

This communication is not merely about stating changes but about creating a space where each partner feels heard, understood, and respected. It's about acknowledging that the person you married years ago may have different needs and desires today and that this evolution is a natural part of the human experience.

Adapting To Each Other's Changing Appetites

Adaptation, then, becomes a vital dance step in the choreography of a long-lasting marriage. It involves not only recognizing and accepting these changes in each other but also finding new ways to connect and fulfill each other's transformed appetites. This might mean redefining intimacy, exploring new hobbies or interests together, or reshaping your lifestyle to align with your current priorities and values.

Ultimately, the changing nature of our appetites is a reminder of the dynamic, ever-evolving journey of marriage. It's about growing together, learning about each other anew, and embracing each phase of life with love, patience, and curiosity.

It's a journey that, when shared with openness and understanding, can deepen the bonds of marriage, turning each new twist and turn into an opportunity for renewed connection and shared joy.

3. Energy levels

As we journey through the chapters of life, our energy levels, much like the ebb and flow of the tides, undergo significant changes. This natural progression is an integral part of the human experience, influencing how we engage with the world and with each other, especially within the bounds of marriage.

Understanding The Cycles Of Energy

The ebbs and flows of our energy are often aligned with the cycles of our life. Just as the seasons change, so too does our vitality and vigor. There is a rhythm, a natural pattern to these shifts, which we must recognize and respect. The exuberant energy of youth, with its boundless enthusiasm and seemingly inexhaustible strength, gradually gives way to the more measured and contemplative pace of later years.

The illustration of the Olympics is a poignant one. The speed and explosive power that characterize the 100-meter finals are the hallmarks of youthful athleticism. It's a spectacle of energy in its most raw and potent form, a domain where youth reigns supreme. This isn't merely a matter of training or willpower; it's a reflection of the natural course of human physiology. As we age, our bodies, and consequently, our energy levels, transform.

This understanding is crucial in the context of marriage. As partners grow and age together, their energy cycles will shift and change. Recognizing and adapting to these changes is key to maintaining harmony and connection. It might mean adjusting expectations around activities and
hobbies and finding new ways to enjoy time together that align with your current energy levels. Perhaps the long hikes or late-night social gatherings of your younger years give way to quieter evenings, gentle walks, or other more serene activities.

Communication And Compassion

Open communication about these changing energy levels is vital. It involves sharing how you're feeling, and what you're capable of, and finding common ground that respects both partners' current states. It's about being compassionate and understanding toward each other, acknowledging that these changes are natural and a part of your shared journey.

Finding Joy In Every Season

Each season of life offers its unique joys and challenges. Embracing the energy of youth is as important as cherishing the more tranquil, reflective energy of later years. In a marriage, this means finding joy and fulfillment in every stage and adapting your activities, goals, and lifestyle to the rhythm of your shared life.

Your energy levels may change, but the love and connection you share can remain constant, evolving and adapting to each new chapter of your lives together. In this recognition and adaptation lies the beauty of a long-lasting, fulfilling marriage.

The Shifting Sands of Interests

Journey through the years of marriage, and you'll discover that the landscape of your interests, much like a garden through the seasons, undergoes its own transformation. These shifts in what captures our attention and ignites our passion are not just inevitable, but they are also signs of personal growth and evolution.

Consider the example of my love for soccer as a younger person, a passion that once dictated schedules and sparked lively discussions. This interest, which once held a central place in my life, has now simmered down to a gentle ember, still warm but no longer the blazing fire it used to be. The players who were once heroes in my eyes are just names from the past, no longer a topic that stirs up excitement even though I sometimes relive the memories of their soccer artistry.

Such changes in interests are a natural part of the journey. As we age, our priorities shift, our perspectives widen, and what fascinated us in the past may no longer hold the same allure. This evolution is not a loss but a sign of our dynamic nature as human beings.

Navigating Changes in Interests within Marriage

In the context of marriage, these evolving interests represent an opportunity for renewed connection and discovery. It's essential to keep track of not only our changing passions but also those of our partners. Just as software needs updates to stay relevant and functional, so do we need to update our understanding of each other's interests to maintain the liveliness of our relationship too?

This process involves open communication and shared exploration. It's about expressing curiosity about your partner's new hobbies or passions and inviting them to participate in yours. It's a journey of continuous discovery, where you both take turns leading and following in the dance of mutual interest.

The Bond Of Shared And Individual Passions

Finding a balance between shared interests and individual passions is key. While it's important to have activities you enjoy together, respecting and supporting each other's interests is equally as important. This balance ensures that both partners feel fulfilled and valued, both together and apart.

Embracing The New

As interests evolve, so too should the activities and conversations within a marriage. This might mean replacing the ritual of watching a soccer match together with a new activity that resonates with both of you now. It's about being open to exploring new territories together, and finding joy and connection in new experiences.

The changing nature of our interests is a reminder of our ongoing journey of growth and exploration. In a marriage, it offers a canvas for painting new experiences, for sharing and learning, and for continuously rediscovering each other. It's about embracing change, not as a challenge, but as an opportunity to deepen and enrich the variety of your shared life. In navigating the ever-changing terrain of marriage, the key lies not just in recognizing the shifts in beliefs, energy levels, interests, and other aspects of life, but also in adeptly crafting strategies to adapt to these changes. The essence of a resilient and fulfilling marriage is the ability to turn these evolving dynamics into opportunities that enrich, rather than diminish, the bond you share.

Weaving Tailored Strategies For Change

Each area of change – beliefs, energy, interests, and more – demands its unique approach. There is no one-size-fits-all strategy, as each couple's journey is distinct. The art lies in identifying these shifts as they emerge and responding in a way that aligns with both partners' current needs and aspirations.

1. Recognizing and Embracing Change

The first step is awareness. This involves being attuned not only to your own evolving preferences and capacities but also to those of your partner. Regular, open conversations about how each of you is feeling and changing are important. This doesn't just strengthen understanding but also reinforces the sense of teamwork in beating life's ebbs and flows together.

2. Influencing the Season

Once changes are recognized, the next step is to influence these 'seasons' of change to your advantage. This might mean finding new activities that align with your current energy levels, exploring new areas of interest together, or even redefining your relationship dynamics to match your evolved belief systems.

3. Maintaining the Emotional Connection

Amidst these changes, it's best to keep the emotional connection alive. This might involve creating new rituals or traditions that resonate with your current selves, finding new ways to express love and appreciation, or simply spending quality time together in ways that reflect your current interests and energy levels.

4. Adapting with Flexibility and Openness

Flexibility and openness are your allies in this journey. Being willing to let go of old patterns that no longer serve you and embracing new ways of being together can lead to a more fulfilling and dynamic relationship. It's about writing your story together with a pen that's willing to adapt its ink to the paper of the present.

The strategy for each of these areas differs but the most important response is to be able to recognize the issues and create a strategy to influence the season to your advantage in such a way that it doesn't affect what you both feel for each other.

Recognize The Changes

Recognizing changes in your marriage, especially those that arrive without warning, is a critical skill that can greatly influence how you both go through different seasons of life. Being proactive and prepared to lead through these changes, rather than being led by them, can make a significant difference in maintaining a healthy and fulfilling relationship.

Consider the scenario where one partner suddenly steps into the limelight, gaining recognition and a following that they didn't have before. This newfound fame can significantly impact both the individual and the relationship. As the partner of someone who's now in the public eye, it's essential to acknowledge and understand the responsibilities and pressures that come with this new status.

STRATEGIES FOR ADAPTING TO NEW DYNAMICS IN THIS SITUATION:

A. Seek Understanding and Be Supportive: It's essential to recognize that your spouse's new role will bring about changes in their life and, by extension, your relationship. Be supportive and understanding of their commitments and the adjustments they need to make.

B. Find Reliable Mentors: Seeking guidance from mentors who have gone through similar paths can be invaluable. They can provide insights and strategies for coping with the changes and maintaining a strong relationship despite external pressures.

C. Open Communication: Sit down together and discuss the impact of these changes on your relationship openly. Conversations should address how both of you feel about these developments, the potential challenges you foresee, and strategies to overcome them. It's important to create a safe space where both partners feel heard and understood.

D. Plan Together: Develop a plan to manage these new dynamics. This might include setting aside quality time, establishing boundaries to protect your relationship, and finding ways to stay connected amidst busy schedules.

E. Embrace the Change Together: Rather than viewing the change as an individual's journey, approach it as a shared adventure. Celebrate the successes together and work as a team to overcome the challenges.

F. Stay Grounded: In times of significant change, it's easy to lose sight of the foundational elements that made your relationship strong. Remind each other of your shared values, goals, and the love that brought you together.

G. Be Flexible and Adapt: Be prepared to adapt to changing circumstances. Flexibility and the willingness to modify your plans and expectations can be crucial in successfully navigating this new phase of your life.

Change, especially when it's sudden and significant, can test a marriage. However, by recognizing these changes, communicating openly, seeking guidance, and planning together, you can turn these challenges into opportunities for growth and deeper connection. Remember, it's not just about navigating change but about growing through it together.

Engaging actively and positively with the changes your spouse is experiencing is crucial for maintaining a healthy and harmonious relationship. It's about understanding that when your partner evolves or their interests shift, it's not just an individual transformation but a development that affects the whole relationship.

EMBRACING YOUR PARTNER'S CHANGING WORLD MAY INVOLVE THE FOLLOWING:

A. Assess the Consequences of Disinterest: Reflect on what might happen if you choose to remain disengaged from your spouse's new interests or changes. Often, neglecting the need to show interest in what matters to them can lead to feelings of distance and disconnection. This detachment can have a ripple effect, causing a rift in your marital bond.

B. Show Genuine Curiosity: One of the most effective ways to get interested in your spouse's changes is to cultivate genuine curiosity. Ask questions about their new interests, hobbies, or the changes they are going through. This shows that you care about their world and are willing to be part of it.

C. Participate in Their World: Take a step further by actively participating in their interests. This could mean joining them in their new hobby, attending events related to their interests, or simply setting aside time to talk about what excites them. Sharing in their world strengthens the bond and enhances mutual understanding.

D. Understand the Importance of Shared Experiences: Shared experiences are the bedrock of a strong relationship. By getting involved in your spouse's new world, you create shared memories and experiences, which are vital for a thriving marriage.

E. Prioritize Marital Harmony: Keeping the peace and harmony in your marriage should be a priority.

If engaging with your partner's changes contributes to a more harmonious relationship, it's undoubtedly a worthwhile investment.

F. Balance Between Individuality and Togetherness: While it's essential to show interest in your partner's changes, it's equally important to maintain a balance. Respecting each other's individuality while finding common ground ensures a healthy dynamic where both partners feel valued and understood.

G. Communicate and Compromise: Open communication about how you both can engage with each other's evolving interests is key. There might be instances where compromises are needed, and through healthy communication, you can surpass these together.

Getting interested in the changes your partner is experiencing is not just about appeasing them; it's about actively valuing their growth and development. It's a testament to the depth of your commitment and willingness to journey together through all of life's twists and turns. Remember, the changes in your spouse are not just opportunities for them to grow but are also opportunities for the growth and enrichment of your marriage.

Stick To Your Agreed Routines And Be Loyal To It

Adhering to mutually agreed-upon routines plays a pivotal role in nurturing a healthy, enduring marriage, especially as you go through different life stages together. The routines that once served you well in the pre-childbirth phase of your marriage may need reevaluation and adjustment to accommodate the new dynamics introduced by parenthood.

Adapting Routines To Life's Changing Seasons

A. Reassess and Redefine Routines: Recognize that the

arrival of children marks a significant shift in your marriage. This period necessitates a thoughtful reassessment of your existing routines. Ask yourselves what routines need to evolve or be newly established to suit this chapter of your lives.

B. Jointly Create New Routines: The creation of new routines should be a collaborative effort, reflecting the needs, desires, and realities of both partners. Discuss and agree upon routines that cater to your family's current needs, whether it's about managing household responsibilities, nurturing your relationship, or ensuring personal self-care.

C. Commitment to the Routines: Once these routines are established, commitment to them is crucial. This means being disciplined and consistent in following through, even when it's challenging. Loyalty to these routines signifies respect for the agreement and for each other.

D. Flexibility Within Structure: Commitment to routines is a great step, but maintaining flexibility is just as important. Life with children can be unpredictable, and being able to adapt while keeping the essence of your routines intact is key to managing stress and maintaining harmony.

E. Communicate and Revisit Routines Regularly: Open communication about how well the routines are working (or not) is essential. Be willing to revisit and tweak these routines as your family grows and changes. What works at one stage may not be as effective in another, so regular check-ins and adjustments are beneficial.

F. Balancing Family and Couple Time: Ensure that your routines include dedicated time for nurturing your relationship. Amidst the demands of parenting, it's crucial to keep the romantic and partnership aspect of your relationship alive and well.

G. Lead by Example for Your Children: By sticking to you routines and showing commitment, you not only create a stable environment for your family but also model the values of consistency, teamwork, and adaptability for your children.

In essence, the evolution and adherence to routines in marriage, particularly during significant life transitions like parenthood, are about finding a balance between consistency and adaptability. It's about creating a structure that supports your family's wellbeing, while also leaving room for the spontaneous, unpredictable elements of life. By staying loyal to your agreed routines, you lay a foundation of stability and mutual respect that can support your relationship through all of life's seasons.

Create a feedback system to know if you are both measuring up in the areas of changes. Implementing a robust feedback system within your marriage is a good strategy for managing changes and ensuring both partners are aligned and adapting effectively. This approach, akin to a 'performance review' in the professional world, allows for
regular, structured discussions about how each partner is feeling and coping with the various changes and challenges in your relationship.

Establishing A Feedback System In Marriage

1. Regular Check-Ins: Schedule regular times for open and honest communication. This could be a weekly or monthly 'open day' where you both sit down to discuss how things are going. These check-ins should be considered as important as any other critical appointment in your life.

2. Safe and Open Environment: Create a safe space where both partners feel comfortable sharing their thoughts and feelings. This environment should be free from judgment or defensiveness, where the goal is understanding and growth, not criticism.

3. Specific Feedback: Encourage specific and constructive feedback. Instead of vague comments like "You don't spend enough time with me," use specific instances, such as "I felt lonely when you didn't join me for dinner last Thursday." Specific feedback is more actionable and less likely to be met with defensiveness.

4. Focus on Improvement: The feedback session should not just be about pointing out what's not working, but also about finding ways to improve. Discuss solutions and strategies to address any issues that arise.

5. Active Listening: Both partners should practice active listening – this means fully concentrating on what is being said, understanding it, responding appropriately, and remembering the discussion.

6. Feedback is a Two-Way Call: Ensure that the feedback process is reciprocal. Both partners should have the opportunity to speak and be heard.

7. Celebrate Progress: Acknowledge and celebrate improvements and progress in your relationship. Recognizing positive changes can be incredibly motivating and reinforcing.

8. Adjusting Based on Feedback: Be prepared to make changes based on the feedback received. This may involve adjusting behaviors, routines, or even the way you communicate with each other.

9. Professional Guidance if Needed: If there are issues that seem too complex to handle alone, don't hesitate to seek professional guidance from a marriage counselor or therapist. Incorporating a feedback system into your marriage is about proactively managing the relationship and ensuring both partners are on the same page. It's a tool for growth, adaptation, and mutual understanding, allowing you to navigate life's changes together more effectively. Remember, the strongest marriages are those where continuous improvement and open communication are embraced.

Patiently explain some changes that may not be so easy to adjust to and give your partner a chance to adjust Going through the changes in a marriage requires patience and understanding, particularly when these changes challenge deeply ingrained habits or personality traits. Recognizing that each individual adjusts at their own pace is key to fostering a supportive and compassionate relationship.

Cultivating Patience In Times Of Change

A. Empathetic Communication: When discussing changes that are challenging to adjust to, approach the conversation with empathy. Recognize that what might seem a minor adjustment to you could be significant for your partner. Patiently explain why this change is essential and how it can benefit both of you and your relationship.

B. Acknowledge the Difficulty: Validating the difficulty of adjusting to certain changes can be comforting for your partner. Acknowledge that it's not always easy to let go of familiar ways or adapt to new ones, especially when these are closely tied to one's personality or long-standing habits.

C. Provide Time to Adjust: Understand that adaptation is a process, not an event. Give your partner time to assimilate and adjust to the new changes. Avoid pressuring them to adapt quickly, as this can lead to frustration and resistance.

D. Offer Support and Guidance: Be there to support your partner through this transition. Offer help, guidance, and encouragement. Sometimes, just knowing that they have your support can make a significant difference in how they approach the change.

E. Set Realistic Expectations: Be realistic in your expectations regarding how quickly and effectively changes can be integrated. Setting overly ambitious goals can lead to disappointment and discouragement.

F. Celebrate Small Wins: Recognize and celebrate even the smallest progress. This positive reinforcement can motivate your partner to continue making efforts to adjust.

G. Practice Active Listening: Listen actively to your partner's concerns and feelings about the changes. Sometimes, just having a safe space to express themselves can make the process of adaptation smoother.

H. Maintain a Positive Attitude: Keeping a positive and hopeful attitude can be infectious. If your partner sees that you're optimistic about the changes and their ability to adjust, it can boost their confidence and willingness to try.

I. Seek External Support if Needed: If the changes are particularly challenging and impact your relationship significantly, don't hesitate to seek external support from a counselor or therapist. Professional guidance can provide the tools and strategies needed to manage the change more effectively.

Patience and understanding are crucial when dealing with changes in a marriage, especially those that are not easily adjusted to. Remember that your partner is not a robot but a human with emotions and limitations. By providing a supportive environment, being patient, and offering encouragement, you can navigate these changes together, strengthening your bond in the process,

Stay Committed to Achieving Your Desired Marital Outcomes

In the Triangle of Life strategy model that I employ with my clients, we focus on three fundamental components.

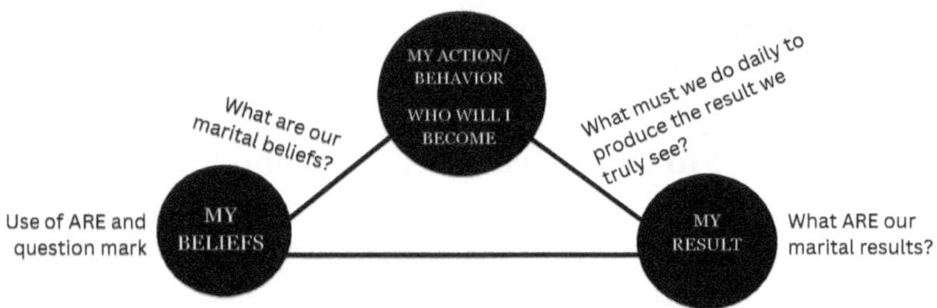

The first part of this triangle is defining the outcomes we desire in our marriage at every stage. Having a clear and defined outcome is important as it serves as the foundation upon which we can build and adjust our efforts to achieve the results we seek. For instance, let's consider the desired outcome of 'marital bliss powered by deep friendships.'

Once we've established our desired outcome, the next step is to adopt the beliefs that can lead us toward those outcomes. Regardless of external circumstances, our beliefs must guide our actions. Using the example above, a relevant belief might be, 'My spouse is a cherished partner who always has my best interests at heart.'

The most challenging part of this process is embracing the actions or behaviors required to realize our desired results. This often involves making changes in our behavior and becoming the person we need to be to truly achieve those outcomes. Our egos can resist this change because it may require us to shift from what we are comfortable with to what is necessary.

To put these beliefs into action, we need to establish routines and rituals that support the desired outcomes. For instance, in the example above, this might involve activities such as maintaining a daily spousal gratitude journal, holding a weekly open day for honest communication, and having a weekly movie night or any other activity that fosters the deep friendships needed to promote marital bliss.

The concept of continuous development in a marriage is pivotal for maintaining a vibrant and fulfilling relationship. Couples who master this art understand the importance of evolving together, adapting to each other's growth, and reinventing themselves to stay attuned to their partner's changing needs and desires. This ongoing process ensures that the connection remains strong, and the mutual attraction endures over time.

Key Aspects Of Continuous Development In Marriage:

1. Reinvention and Relevance: Successful couples recognize
that staying relevant in each other's lives often requires a
process of reinvention. This could involve developing new
interests, learning new skills, or even changing certain behaviors to align better with each other's evolving needs.

2. Maintaining Vibrations: Keeping the level of vibrations intact is about ensuring that the emotional and intellectual connection between partners remains lively and engaging. This involves ongoing communication, shared experiences, and a deep understanding of each other's evolving passions and perspectives.

3. Adapting to Growth: Both partners in a marriage are likely to grow and change over time. Recognizing and supporting each other's personal growth is crucial. This support can be through encouragement, showing interest in their new pursuits, or even participating in learning and growth opportunities together.

4. Innovation in Relationship Dynamics: Continuous development also means being innovative in how you relate to each other. This might mean finding new ways to express love, experimenting with different forms of date nights, or adopting new communication strategies to deepen your connection.

5. Embracing Change as an Opportunity: Change is inevitable in any long-term relationship. Couples who thrive see these changes not as obstacles but as opportunities to deepen their understanding and appreciation for each other.

6. Proactive Approach: A proactive approach to continuous development involves anticipating and planning for potential changes or challenges. This might include discussing future goals, preparing for different life stages, or even seeking professional advice when needed.

7. Regular Assessments: Just as businesses conduct regular reviews to gauge progress, successful couples often assess their relationship. This might involve discussing what is working well, what needs improvement, and setting goals for the future.

In essence, continuous development in a marriage is about maintaining a dynamic, responsive, and proactive approach to the relationship. It's about growing individually and together, ensuring that the bond not only survives but thrives through the various phases of life. By staying attuned to each other's needs, desires, and dreams, and being willing to adapt and grow, couples can keep their relationship vibrant and fulfilling for years to come.

End Note Reflection Questions.

1. How have we both changed since the beginning of our relationship and in what ways have we adapted our routines and interactions to accommodate these changes?

2. In what areas do we need to reinvent ourselves or our relationship to stay relevant and connected to each other?

3. How effectively do we communicate and navigate changes in our interests, beliefs, and energy levels? Where can we improve?

4. What new routines, rituals, or activities can we introduce to strengthen our bond and keep our relationship vibrant and engaging?

5. Reflecting on the concept of continuous development, how can we be more supportive and understanding of each other's personal growth and changes?

CHAPTER 10

Strategy

I often like to draw a parallel between a marriage and a football team competing in a league, year after year, with the clear agenda of building a peaceful world. One fundamental lesson every successful team understands is that the quality of players, their ability to work together as a team, and employing superior playing patterns and tactical formations are key to winning matches.

In marriage, ignorance of your own relationship's 'playing pattern' is akin to setting yourself up for failure. Equally critical is the lack of understanding about your partner's tactics and how to counter them. Just as in sports, where matches aren't solely won by having superior players, but by superior strategy, marriage hinges on having the right strategies for the right seasons.

Even the best intentions and righteousness may not suffice if you are unaware of the tactical formation required for victory.
I occasionally conduct pre-marital counseling workshops, and it never fails to amuse me to see the unrealistic expectations and excitement of soon-to-be-wedded couples. They often have no inkling of the level of crisis management that successful marriages often entail.

I've consistently emphasized that the most crucial ingredient in building a successful marriage is 'Applied Knowledge.' There are seasons in a marriage that can make or break it, and without a deep understanding of the season you're in, you might find yourself on the brink of separation.

In 2021, I worked with Debbie and her husband when they were teetering on the edge of divorce. Her husband reluctantly sought my services. After our third session together, Debbie sent me this email:

Dear Praise,

I hardly know where to begin, for the transformation we've experienced in just three sessions feels nothing short of miraculous. What's truly astonishing is that you haven't handed us a checklist of do's and don'ts, as you initially mentioned when we embarked on this journey.

Instead, you've opened our eyes to what we've overlooked for so many years, and it turns out these oversights were the very reasons we were on the verge of separation.

I've always believed that God would bless us with a good marriage, but never once did I associate the term 'strategy' with matrimony. I work as a project manager, and I understand the significance of strategy in scenario planning. However, I never fathomed that it could be applied to marriage until our recent session.

For the first time, I saw numerous situations in which we both could have turned the tide if we'd only recognized the need for the right strategy. I also realized how many unnecessary conflicts I had entangled myself in when a well-thought-out strategy could have smoothed the way.

My husband hails from Ghana, as you know, and dealing with my mother-in-law has been a major issue. I had consistently felt unloved and unaccepted as a Black

American. However, after our last session, a profound revelation struck me. I hadn't made any sincere effort to connect because I was too focused on imposing my own style and values. However following your guidance on the strategy elicitation model, I decided to take a different approach.

To my amazement, it worked wonders. For the first time, my mother-in-law reached out to me, suggesting that we spend time together. My husband's siblings are suddenly warming up to me, and my husband himself seems happier than ever. It's as if we've rediscovered each other.

Thank you for everything you do. You've truly been a lifesaver.

Warm regards,

Debbie

Every Problem Has Solutions

Every problem indeed carries within itself the seeds of its own solution, waiting for those willing to delve deep enough to uncover them. Here, let's infuse a touch of inspiration into your piece. Within the context of family life, challenges often emerge as unwelcome guests. Yet, amidst the trials, there exists hope - the solution. It is a reassuring truth that every problem, no matter how daunting, is accompanied by its remedy. The irony lies in the fact that this remedy is frequently concealed within the very depths of the problem itself, awaiting discovery by those who dare to delve.

In family life, we family professionals are akin to both therapists and coaches. Our clients, seeking solace amidst life's tumultuous seas, often yearn for swift resolutions. In their hearts, there's no distinction between therapist and coach; they simply seek help, a lifeline amidst the turbulence.

Each marriage, like the ever-changing seasons, journeys through its unique cycles. In the symphony of matrimony, couples build complex of strategies, each tailored to a different note of their life's composition. Yet, within the diversity of strategies, a remarkable breakthrough emerges - the capacity to distill successes into strategic frameworks. This transformational ability breathes life into our organization, equipping us to cultivate playbooks for myriad situations.

As an organization, we have forged these playbooks, each a treasure trove of wisdom and solutions. Yet, we remain vigilant, ready to adapt and evolve as the tides of time shift. Within our hallowed strategies, we understand that there are three core pillars of strategy:

Marital Goals/ Bull's Eye: Your Deepest Desires

Within the confines of marriage, it is imperative to chart your course with precision. The marital target or goal is not a vague aspiration; it is the very essence of your shared dreams, distinct and unmistakable.

Imagine desiring a stressless marriage. To manifest this aspiration, we delve deeper, peeling back the layers to reveal the crystal-clear facets of what "stressless" truly means. It's about knowing precisely what it entails – perhaps it's the absence of incessant arguments, the presence of mutual support, or the ability to savor moments of tranquility together. Clarity here is our guiding star.

Going through the Terrain: The Operating Environment In the theater of marriage, we must recognize the rules of engagement, akin to understanding the lay of the land before a grand battle. We embark on an impartial audit of our surroundings and audience.

This is not an emotional reckoning; it's a calculated endeavor to identify stressors lurking in our marital arena. What are the obstacles that, if left unaddressed, could sow the seeds of discord? It's about defining these adversaries and formulating strategies to defuse them. Only through this unemotional examination can we hope to preserve the tranquility of our union

The Crucible Of Internal Capacity

Within this sacred alliance, roles and responsibilities intermingle, converging to form a harmonious symphony. Imagine, for instance, the wife feeling overwhelmed, her burdens of meal preparation and childcare weighing heavily on her. Here, we confront a fundamental query – what roles must we each embrace to bring our vision to life?

The answer lies in the depths of our internal capacity. Are we willing to become the architects of our change? Can the husband step into the role of a culinary collaborator, alleviating the wife's burdens? Or, do we need to expand our horizons and consider hiring a cook to ease the load? A key element here is feasibility; can we afford such an investment in our shared happiness?

Ultimately, this is a reflection of who we aspire to become within this union. It's about transformation, about evolving into versions of ourselves that can actively and willingly contribute to the realization of our shared dreams.

In the strategic framework of marriage, these three pillars – the Marital Bullseye, Operating Environment, and Internal Capacity – fuse harmoniously. With precision, we aim for our desires. With clarity, we navigate the challenges of our surroundings. And with unwavering determination, we fortify our internal capacities.

Together, these facets illuminate the path to a marriage that thrives, where dreams are not mere shadows but tangible, shared realities.

Harmonizing Hearts: A Case Study Strategy for Peaceful Coexistence. Amidst the reality of cultures and emotions, Kate found herself entangled in a difficult relationship with her Nigerian mother-inlaw.

The toxicity of this connection had begun to corrode the bonds of her marriage, leaving her yearning for a solution that would breathe serenity back into her world.

In our quest to resolve this conundrum, we embarked on a structured journey, drawing upon the three essential facets of strategic intervention: the Marital Target, Operating Environment, and Internal Capacity.

1. Marital Target: Cultivating Tranquil Coexistence The end game of our strategy was unequivocally clear – to nurture a relationship of harmonious coexistence with Kate's mother-in-law. This aspiration was not a vague wish but a well-defined beacon of serenity, a vision of two hearts finding common ground within their cultural diversity.

2. Operating Environment: Navigating Optics and Opportunities

To reframe this fraught relationship, we embarked on an impartial reconnaissance of the battlefield – the operating environment. This analytical exploration involved dissecting the dynamics, perceptions, and potential pathways for transformation.

We discerned opportunities to mend the fractures – family gatherings shared festivities, and moments of unity where the common thread of love could be rewoven. By understanding the landscape, we unearthed channels to connect on a deeper level, gently navigating the tricky terrain of in-law dynamics.

3. Internal Capacity: A Guiding Acronym. The third facet of our strategy was an ingenious acronym designed to serve as

Kate's code of engagement – a compass for her interactions with her mother-in-law. We created two different acronyms that encapsulated her guiding principles, spelling out the path to reconciliation

The first acronym, **P.R.A.I.S.E,** is a wonderful guideline for building positive relationships and showing respect.

P -Praise Her: Always find opportunities to offer praise, even when you may not immediately see something praiseworthy. Acknowledging her efforts, no matter how small, can strengthen your bond.

R -Readily Respond Respectfully: Respond promptly and respectfully to her intentions and actions. Show appreciation for her contributions, no matter how insignificant they may seem.

A -Acknowledge Her Input: Recognize her input and impact
in your life, even if her role has primarily been as your husband's mother. Every individual brings something unique to the family dynamic.

I - Interview and Learn: Take the time to interview her, not just as a formality but to genuinely understand her culture and worldview. Consider her as a potential mentor who can offer valuable insights.

S - Solve Problems Swiftly With Speed and Smile: When she faces challenges, address them with speed and a smile. Being proactive in helping her resolve issues demonstrates your care and consideration.

E -Exceed Expectations: Go above and beyond to exceed her expectations. Surpassing what she anticipates can foster a deep sense of connection and appreciation.

This acronym encapsulates a powerful approach to building positive relationships, especially within the context of extended family dynamics.

The other acronym I recommended was the LOVEUR model:

- **Learn:** To truly understand her mother-in-law, Kate committed to learning about Nigerian customs, traditions, and values.

- **Openness:** She chose the path of openness, embracing conversations that allowed for mutual understanding.

- **Vulnerability:** Kate decided to reveal her authentic self, acknowledging her own vulnerabilities and fears.

- **Empathy:** Empathy became her cornerstone, seeking to see the world through her mother-in-law's eyes.

- **Unity:** The ultimate aim was unity, uniting as a family rather than as adversaries.

- **Respect:** Mutual respect, borne from cultural appreciation, became the linchpin of their interaction.

With these guiding acronyms, Kate embarked on a transformative journey towards bridging the cultural chasm between them. Through strategic clarity, Kate found the compass to navigate the intricate labyrinth of family dynamics. This was not just a strategy for resolution; it was a roadmap for healing, an ode to building bridges, and a testament to the power of love transcending borders and differences.

So a breakdown of our strategy looks like this

MARITAL GOAL	OPERATING ENVIRONMENT	INTERNAL CAPACITY
Build a peaceful co-existing relationship with mother inlaw	• She loves those that understand her language. • She is a control freak and wants to feel recognized. • Shares a good bond with husband • She loves her only daughter whom I can create a rapport with. • Change my beliefs from wicked woman to amazing mother	**P-** praise her always **R-** readily respond respectfully to her intentions **A-** acknowledge her input and impact no matter how little **I -** Interest and interview her to learn something new **S-** solve her problem with speed and smile **E-** exceed her expectations

"In the span of just seven months, she had not only achieved our goal but had surpassed it to the point where even the most critical in-law couldn't do without her.

This underscores a fundamental truth: when we shift the way we perceive things and align our actions with our beliefs, the desired results become inevitable. In navigating the complexities of various scenarios, we have two potent tools at our disposal: the 3-Strategy Pillar Model and the Triangle of Life Matrix. These frameworks empower us to resolve even the most intricate issues effectively.

"In any situation we face, it's essential to realize that we possess the capabilities needed to triumph, provided we can craft the right winning formula. When creating a strategic system, we must keep the following principles in mind:

Strategies are not emotional; they are only loyal to outcomes. In strategies, emotions take a back seat, for they are but servants to the desired outcome. As the English Premier League graces the world with its soccer spectacle, a notable maestro, Pep Guardiola, has brought a new style to Manchester City making them a formidable force. Their passing game has left many in awe, yet a select few have successfully pierced their armor.

These valiant opponents didn't tread the path of blind adoration for the beautiful game; instead, they understood that strategies must be as fluid as water, loyal not to personal preferences, but to the conquest of victory. A clash with Pep's team demanded not mimicry, but adaptation – a tactical metamorphosis.

In the same vein, familial customs are often deeply embedded in the cultural nuances of a society. Take, for instance, the African tradition of unannounced visits, an expression of warmth and community. Yet, in the Western world, personal privacy is revered as sacrosanct.

To harmonize these distinct worlds within your family, the compass of strategy guides your steps, regardless of personal sentiment. It's a journey through uncharted territory, marked by decisions that may bewilder even those you cherish most. The key is to remain resolute, for strategic clarity transcends momentary discomfort.

Consider a scenario where the desire is to shield your family's private sanctum in a culture accustomed to unannounced visits. This strategic blueprint necessitates firmly declining unexpected guests, despite initial misunderstandings. The heartaches of these rejections become stepping stones to a family culture that values and preserves personal privacy.

In the art of strategy, emotions must bow to the master plan. Just as teams adapt to conquer, families evolve to thrive. It's the tactical impersonal dance where the desired outcome reigns supreme, guiding every step towards a future where victory is not just a possibility, but a certainty.

2. Strategic systems make life intentional- Life unfurls like a vast, uncharted wilderness, and without a strategic plan, we're but wanderers, carried by the winds of chance. It's akin to playing chess without a strategy - a surefire path to failure. The adage warns that those who fail to plan often plan to fail, but here's the finer point: if you lack a strategic blueprint for success, you're unwittingly devising a strategy for failure.

In the game of strategy, life transcends mere existence; it becomes intentional. It's akin to crafting a masterpiece, where every brushstroke is deliberate, every note, harmonious. A strategic plan acts as the compass, guiding you through the labyrinth of existence. With it, you become the architect of your destiny, the composer of your symphony.

Strategies are the alchemists of life, capable of transforming dreams into reality. They enable you to audit your ambitions, scrutinize your internal capacities, and decipher the nuances of your operating environment. In essence, they illuminate the path ahead, revealing the potential pitfalls, the detours, and the shortcuts to your goals.

Imagine a scenario where a strategic plan foresees a period of separation in your family life, say, in the 12th year of marriage. Instead of blindly stumbling into the chasm of separation, you face it with intent. Questions arise, like sparks in the night:

- How will this affect our marriage?
- What impact will it have on our parenting?
- How can we nurture our children to be independent
- thinkers before this juncture?
- What safeguards must be erected to ensure nothing goes awry?

In the intricate dance of life, strategy serves as your choreographer. It not only poses these questions but also provides well-rehearsed answers. It carves out the path, determining the steps you need to take, and the moves you need to master.

In essence, strategic systems grant life the gift of intentionality.

They render the canvas of existence a masterpiece in the making, each stroke deliberates, and each note is played with purpose. With a clear strategy, life unfolds as a journey worth living, where success is not a matter of chance but a destiny woven into the very fabric of your being.

3. Strategy deploys overt communication and behavior to win covert battles – Marriage, they say, is a crucible of crisis management, where strategic battles, though often hidden, shape the course of a relationship. To master this delicate art, one must understand that success is not solely contingent upon the clarity of your desires but equally reliant on a deftly crafted communication and actualization plan tailored to your partner's understanding.

In the grand theater of marriage, you don't assert your rights; you perform what is right for your union. It's akin to the wisdom of the great Jewish philosopher, Paul of Tarsus, who proclaimed, "I became all things to all men so that I can convert them." This
transformation entails using overt expressions to conquer
covert battles, where the overt represents the language your
partner comprehends, and the covert is the true outcome you
seek.

Let's illustrate this with a tale of love and an old, wobbly chair. Picture a woman upset by her husband's unwavering loyalty to a chair with a precarious leg, gifted to him by his late father. She knows that convincing him to part with it is a Herculean task, yet it poses a safety hazard. Instead of engaging in futile arguments, she orchestrates an artful overture.

In secret, she plans a surprise party, inviting cherished friends and an old schoolmate known for their playful rivalry. As the gathering unfolds, she publicly extols her husband's virtues, showering him with praise and appreciation. Then, with a gentle touch of finesse, she subtly raises a question: *"Is there anything in our sitting room that might send the wrong message to our guests about our family?"* The magic happens. He identifies the chair, realizing its incongruity with the celebratory ambiance. Without resistance, he orders a set of new chairs, even refurbishing his beloved relic for the study, where it holds sentimental value.

This ingenious approach embodies the art of strategic orchestration. By skillfully crafting an overt conversation, she transcended his conscious defenses and achieved her covert objective. It's a testament to the power of strategy in navigating the intricate terrain of marriage, where battles won through artistry often yield the sweetest victories.

Reflection Questions

1. Reflect on Your Personal Strategy: What specific strategies have you employed in your own life, whether in relationships, career, or personal growth, and how have they influenced your outcomes?

2. Understanding Purpose and Outcomes: In your opinion, how crucial is having a clear purpose and desired outcome when crafting a strategy for any area of life, including marriage and family?

3. Embracing Adaptation: Can you recall a situation where you had to adapt or change your strategy due to unforeseen circumstances? What did you learn from this experience?

4. Balancing Emotional and Strategic Decisions: How do you strike a balance between making emotionally driven decisions and strategically sound ones, especially in personal relationships like marriage?

5. The Power of Effective Communication: Share an instance from your life where skillful communication helped you achieve a desired outcome or resolve a conflict strategically. What did you learn from that experience?

CULTIVATE TRUST AND HONESTY

> *Trust is the cornerstone of a lasting marriage. Be trustworthy and transparent in your actions, fostering a deep sense of security and intimacy.*

CHAPTER 11

Technical Crew

In the world of the English Premier League, one name stands out as a master of the game: Sir Alex Ferguson, the legendary former manager of Manchester United. His leadership catapulted the team to the pinnacle of English football, earning them a place in history. Yet, the tale of his succession is one of caution.

Manchester United, once a dominant force, witnessed a sudden decline in fortunes after Sir Alex's retirement. The blame lay partially on the choice of his successor, a decision that left fans and critics bewildered. The Glazer family, who acquired the club, seemed more interested in its commercial success than its footballing legacy.

Consequently, the appointment of David Moyes, a coach with limited accolades and no high-level success, raised eyebrows.
In fairness, a coach need not have a glittering playing career to excel, but such exceptions are rare and usually involve individuals with exceptional tactical prowess. Moyes, while not inept, was akin to a level 4 coach leading a level 1 team. This leadership mismatch devastated the team's cohesion and performance, leading to his eventual dismissal.

However, a lesser-known leadership error occurred during Moyes' tenure. Sir Alex Ferguson's trusted technical assistants, the guardians of Manchester United's footballing traditions, were in place, offering invaluable knowledge and continuity.

Moyes, regrettably, chose to part ways with them. He brought in his own team, loyal but unaccustomed to the demands of a top-tier team. The results were, to put it mildly, disappointing.
Subsequent lessons were learned from this debacle. Teams began to promote from within or recruit established winners to helm their campaigns. The choice of a technical crew became pivotal.

Coaches, like teams, have ratings. Some are sought after by elite clubs, others by mid-level teams, and a few are perpetually hired by relegation battlers. Marriages, we found, share this trait. To ensure marital success, couples must not entrust their union to just anyone; they must choose their *"technical crew"* wisely. Interdependence...

Human beings are not designed for complete independence; we thrive through interdependence. We need each other, for when isolation looms, our worst instincts can surface.

Absolute power corrupts absolutely. Abusive relationships often lack authority figures to provide guidance and restraint. Marital disputes and clashing egos may necessitate a credible third party. If your partner lacks mentors, leaders, or parents who can offer guidance, you might be partnering with a *"beast."* Unless, of course, they've invested heavily in personal growth.

Your technical crew need not be someone married for decades; skilled professionals versed in family science can provide a valuable framework. Ideally, find someone combining both theory and practice to guide your journey through the beautiful yet challenging game of marriage.

Your technical crew is the team of coaches that can help you win in your marriage, and these coaches must possess certain qualities:

1. Experienced Playmakers: Look for individuals who have overcome the ups and downs of life's journey, especially in the realm of relationships. Their experience can provide valuable insights when you face challenging moments.

2. Effective Communicators: Effective communication is the cornerstone of a successful team. Seek coaches who can listen actively, express themselves clearly, and mediate between you and your partner when needed.

3. Emotional Intelligence Experts: Your coaches should be well-versed in understanding emotions, both yours and your partner's. They should guide you in managing emotions constructively rather than destructively.

4. Conflict Resolution Specialists: Marital conflicts are inevitable. Coaches who excel in conflict resolution can teach you techniques to resolve issues without causing lasting damage to your relationship.

5. Goal-Oriented Strategists: Just as in sports, setting goals is crucial in marriage. Your coaches should help you define clear objectives for your relationship and create strategies to achieve them.

6. Empathetic Supporters: Empathy is the glue that binds teams together. Seek coaches who genuinely care about your well-being and understand your unique challenges as a couple.

7. Trustworthy and Reliable: Trust is the foundation of any successful partnership. Ensure that your coaches are trustworthy and can be relied upon for guidance and support.

8. Flexible Adapters: Marriage is dynamic, and strategies that work at one stage may need adjustments later on. Your coaches should be flexible and adaptable to changing circumstances.

9. Holistic Approach: Marriage is not just about one aspect; it encompasses emotional, psychological, and physical elements. Look for coaches who take a holistic approach to your relationship.

10. Cultural Competence: If you come from diverse backgrounds, it's beneficial to have coaches who understand and respect your cultural differences, helping you navigate potential challenges.

11. Supportive Team Players: Your coaches should work seamlessly together and complement each other's strengths. A harmonious coaching team can provide a well-rounded support system.

12. Lifelong Learners: Seek coaches who are committed to continuous learning and self-improvement. They should stay updated with the latest insights and strategies for successful marriages.

In the game of marriage, your technical crew can be your guiding stars. Choose them wisely, and together, you can tackle any challenge and aim for victory in the beautiful journey of matrimony.

1. He must be highly skilled– Every highly effective couple needs a guiding light, a light of wisdom to traverse the delicate paths of our hearts. This guiding light, these maestros of emotion, they are our technical crew, the captains of our romantic odyssey.

Yet, dear friends, we must, however, not tread with the blindfold of naivety. Because the helmsmen of love's vessel must be more than mere dreamers; they must be skilled artisans, honing their craft with dedication and purpose. It is not the native intelligence of trial and error that we seek, but the artistry refined through study and practice.

In this symphony of love, certification is our overture. The credentials of these maestros are their musical notes, their certificates the score by which they compose the harmonious melodies of enduring love stories. To entrust your heart to one who lacks this foundational harmony is akin to sailing on turbulent seas without a map or compass.

Seek clarity, dear lovers, because it is your right. Inquire into the foundations of their knowledge, and trace the lineage of their wisdom. A true master need not hide in obscurity; their mentors and training should shine like stars in the night sky.

Let us not dismiss the value of this pursuit. In the realm of love, where every heartbeat is a precious note, we must ensure that our conductors are maestros who can orchestrate the grandest of symphonies. To settle for less is to risk discord in the most beautiful of compositions.

In the grand opera of love, where hearts are both the audience and the performers, our technical crew must be virtuous.

With clear certifications and the luminous path of mentorship, they can lead us to crescendos of love that resonate through the ages.

2. Respect- In the dance of love and marriage, a guiding hand, wise and revered, is often the compass steering the ship through life's tumultuous seas. Much like a seasoned captain navigating treacherous waters, a couple's journey through matrimony can be profoundly shaped by the presence of a skilled coach but that coach must also be respected.

Imagine this revered guide as a lighthouse, casting its beam of wisdom upon the rocky shores of life. To entrust your marital voyage to such a figure is not merely an option but a vital necessity. This guide, often a skilled professional, is your beacon of hope when storm clouds gather and tempests threaten to tear your union asunder.

The first facet of this esteemed figure is their skill. In matters of the heart, as in any other domain, skill is the foundation upon which everything is built. They are not mere dabblers, experimenting with emotions and human connections. No, they are artisans of the heart, having honed their craft through study, practice, and experience.

Seek out their qualifications, their certifications as I mentioned earlier, because these are the medals of their dedication. A skilled coach does not rely on native intuition alone, because love is a delicate art, requiring both intuition and the wisdom of proven methodologies. They are guided by a clear framework, a treasure map through the labyrinth of emotions and relationships. Their training and mentorship have equipped them to serve as trustworthy custodians of your love story.

However, skill alone is not enough. This guide must command your respect. Picture them as a venerable sage whose words carry the weight of ancient wisdom. When they speak, it is not merely counsel but a symphony of experience and sagacity. Respect is the bridge between knowledge and action. Without it, even the wisest counsel falls on deaf ears. You must both see this guide as someone worthy of deference, someone whose words you'd heed even in the most tumultuous of moments. When respect is the cornerstone, you are less likely to take matters into your own hands, for their guidance is a guiding star in the darkest of nights.

In choosing this revered guide, you are, in essence, inviting a guardian of your love into your innermost sanctum. Their presence is a testament to your commitment, an acknowledgment that your love is worth safeguarding with the utmost care.

So, seek not just a coach, but a maestro of love, skilled and respected because in their hands, your love story becomes a timeless symphony, each note resonating with the harmony of two souls entwined in devotion.

3. Framework and timelines– The role of a coach is akin to that of an architect. They craft the structure of your relationship, ensuring that it stands strong against the winds of time. Yet, it's not enough for them to be creative visionaries; they must also be masters of structure and planning. Thus, a vital aspect of choosing the right coach for your marital journey is their possession of a clear framework and adherence to timelines.

Imagine your love story as a magnificent building, its foundation rooted in shared dreams and aspirations. This structure must not only be beautiful but also functional and enduring. To achieve this, a coach needs a well-defined framework, a blueprint that outlines the path to a lasting and flourishing relationship.

A framework is more than a set of arbitrary rules; it's a

carefully designed roadmap, a treasure trove of methodologies honed through years of experience. It encompasses the principles that guide a couple toward understanding, empathy, and growth. Without this essential framework, a coach is like an architect without a blueprint, relying solely on intuition, which, though valuable, is insufficient in the realm of love.

But what is a blueprint without a timeline? A skilled coach understands the importance of structure in creating lasting change. They recognize that time is both a healer and a revealer, and they utilize it to their advantage.

Timelines provide structure to your journey, setting achievable milestones along the path to a healthier, happier relationship. They help you measure progress, celebrate successes, and navigate challenges. With a clear timeline, you can see the evolution of your love story unfold before your eyes, step by transformative step.

Imagine if a building were constructed without adherence to a timeline; chaos would reign, and the final result might be unstable or incomplete. In the same vein, without a clear plan and timeline, your marital journey could become a disorganized struggle, marked by frustration and uncertainty.
Therefore, when selecting a coach for your marital journey, inquire about their framework and timelines. A skilled professional will gladly share these essential tools with you, demonstrating their commitment to your journey. If their responses leave you uncertain, consider seeking guidance elsewhere, for in the world of love and relationships, structure and timing are the keystones of lasting success. Just as an architect's blueprint guides a masterpiece into existence, your coach's framework and timelines guide your love story toward a future of enduring happiness.

4. Track records– In the journey of love, as in any grand adventure, the proof of a guide's prowess lies not in their words but in the stories of those they've led to success.

Thus, when seeking a coach to illuminate your path in the intricate realm of marriage, the pages of their track records become the most profound chapters to explore. Imagine your quest for or marital bliss as an ancient, boundless vault, filled with tales of love, struggle, and triumph. Within these pages lie the narratives of couples who have walked this path before you, guided by the hand of your prospective coach. To gain insight into your coach's abilities, you must delve into these chronicles and uncover the stories of transformation.

Track records are not mere lists of names and dates; they are the living echoes of past journeys. They reveal the capacity of a coach to breathe life into fading connections and reignite the flames of love. These records bear witness to the strength and wisdom that can be drawn from their guidance.

When you seek a coach, don't be satisfied with their eloquence alone. Words may flow effortlessly from their lips, painting a picture of expertise, but it is in the lived experiences of those they've served that their true colors shine through. To trust in your coach is to trust in the countless stories of love rekindled, bonds strengthened, and lives transformed under their stewardship.

Picture this: an explorer in a foreign land, searching for a guide to lead them through treacherous terrain. Would they not seek the counsel of fellow travelers who have ventured alongside this guide before? In the same vein, when selecting a coach, reach out to those who have trod the same path and inquire about their voyage.

Do not be content with the coach's self-proclaimed successes; venture deeper into the world of testimonials, reviews, and recommendations. Conduct your independent investigation, consult the testimonials of those who have entrusted their hearts to this guide, and unveil the genuine impact of their work.

Just as an explorer would hesitate to traverse uncharted territory, you should be wary of a coach whose track records remain shrouded in obscurity. A true guide, one worthy of your trust, is not afraid to shine a light on the stories of transformation they've woven into the tapestry of love. In many instances, your coach can also serve sometimes as your mentor, your sage, and your companion. Their track records are the footprints of hope etched into the sands of time. Through them, you discover the profound transformations they've orchestrated and the lives they've touched. In these chronicles of love, you unearth the profound testament to their expertise, and it is from these pages that you draw the inspiration to pen your own story of enduring love.

5. Accessibility– Imagine your relationship as a delicate symphony, where every note represents a moment, a question, a concern, or a triumph. In this intricate composition, your coach is the conductor, responsible for guiding each note to create a harmonious melody. Now, picture a conductor who, instead of meticulously orchestrating each note, rushes through the composition, barely pausing to listen to the music. The result? A discordant
cacophony. In the realm of love, a coach who juggles an excessive number of clients without the capacity to provide individual attention risks turning your symphony of love into disarray.

Your coach must be a maestro of accessibility, one who listens attentively to the nuances of your relationship's melody. Love is not a mass-produced tune, and your coach should not treat it as such. Each love story is unique and deserving of personal attention, care, and guidance.

Beware of coaches or mentors who amass an army of clients, leaving their proteges to fend for themselves in a sea of voices. Love's melody requires a conductor who can tune in to its subtleties, adjusting the tempo and volume as needed. When you are left to navigate the complexities of love without your coach's presence, it's akin to performing a symphony without a conductor—notes may be missed, and harmony may elude you.

Imagine, instead, a coach who understands the delicate balance of their role, guiding your love's melody with grace and precision. They are not overwhelmed by a multitude of clients, but rather, they carefully select those they can serve effectively. Accessibility is their anthem, and your relationship is their masterpiece.

In love's symphony, accessibility is the key to harmonious progress. Your coach should be readily available to listen, guide, and nurture your unique love story. They must provide the space for your questions, fears, and joys to be heard and addressed.

As you embark on your journey of love, remember that your relationship is a symphony—a work of art in progress. The conductor you choose should be attuned to your melody, skilled in their craft, and available to fine-tune your love's composition. In their accessibility, you find the assurance that every note of your love story will be cherished and conducted with care.

6. Professional fees – Love, they say, is priceless. It's an emotion that knows no bounds, transcending time and circumstance. But in the reality of relationships, there's a practical aspect to consider—your coach's professional fees. This is the investment you make to safeguard and enrich the most precious aspect of your life: your love story.

Imagine your love as a magnificent garden, a place where dreams take root and emotions bloom. Now, picture your coach as the guardian of this garden, nurturing the soil, tending to the delicate petals, and ensuring its continued growth and beauty.

Just as a garden requires care and attention, your relationship deserves the same. In your journey of love, your coach is a skilled gardener who knows the secrets of cultivating lasting love. They possess the knowledge, tools, and expertise to help your love blossom and flourish. And like any gardener, they relationship through your coach's professional fees is a declaration of your commitment to nurturing the love you cherish.

Professional fees are not a mere transaction; they are a testament to the value you place on your love story. Your coach is not just a mentor; they are your partner in crafting a love that withstands the tests of time. Their guidance can help you navigate the thorns and brambles that may threaten to choke your love's growth.

It's essential to budget for your coach's fees because they bring an invaluable treasure to your relationship—knowledge. With each session, you gain insights, strategies, and wisdom that empower you to overcome challenges and savor the sweetest moments of love. This investment paves the way for a deeper connection, a stronger bond, and a love that endures.

Think of your coach's professional fees as the water that quenches your love's thirst and the sunlight that bathes it in warmth. It's the fertilizer that enriches the soil of your relationship and the protective barrier that shields it from the storms of life.

In love, as in life, investments yield returns. When you invest in your relationship through your coach's professional fees, you are sowing the seeds of a love that will bear the most beautiful and enduring fruits. Your love story is a garden worthy of the finest care, and your coach is the guardian who can make it flourish.

Having a technical crew, a team of skilled professionals, in your corner when it comes to your marriage can be a game-changer.

Here are some of the benefits of having a technical crew in creating a highly effective and successful marriage:

1. Expert Guidance: Your technical crew consists of experts in various aspects of relationships, from communication to conflict resolution. They bring a wealth of knowledge and experience to help you navigate challenges effectively.

2. Objective Perspective: These professionals can provide an objective perspective on your relationship. They aren't emotionally involved, which allows them to offer unbiased advice and solutions.

3. Conflict Resolution: One of the primary roles of your technical crew is to help you resolve conflicts. They can teach you healthy ways to address disagreements and prevent them from escalating into major issues.

4. Improved Communication: Effective communication is at the heart of any successful marriage. Your technical crew can teach you and your partner better communication skills, helping you understand each other more deeply.

5. Emotional Support: Marriage can be emotionally challenging at times. Your technical crew can provide emotional support and a safe space to express your feelings and concerns.

6. Customized Strategies: Your technical crew can develop customized strategies and action plans tailored to your unique relationship dynamics and goals.

7. Prevention of Issues: They can help you identify potential issues before they become major problems. By addressing issues early, you can prevent them from damaging your relationship.

8. Accountability: Your technical crew can hold both you and your partner accountable for your actions and commitments. This accountability can help you stay on track with your goals.

9. Strengthened Bond: With the guidance of your technical crew, you can work on strengthening your emotional connection and intimacy, leading to a deeper bond.

10. Long-Term Success: Ultimately, having a technical crew increases your chances of long-term success in your marriage. They provide you with the tools and strategies you need to build in resilient and fulfilling partnership.

Your technical crew plays a crucial role in creating a highly effective marriage by offering expert guidance, resolving conflicts, improving communication, providing emotional support, and helping you achieve your relationship goals. They are an invaluable resource for couples committed to building a strong and lasting marriage.

Reflection Questions

1. Reflect on your current approach to addressing challenges in your marriage. Have you considered seeking professional guidance, or have you relied solely on your own resources? Who can you sign up with as your marital coach?

2. Think about your communication patterns with your spouse. Are there areas where you struggle to communicate effectively?

How can improved communication benefit your relationship?
3. Consider past conflicts in your marriage. How were they resolved, and were the outcomes satisfactory? How can a skilled professional assist in resolving conflicts more constructively?

4. What are your long-term goals for your marriage? How do you envision your relationship in the future? How can a technical crew help you work toward these goals?

5. Reflect on your willingness to invest time and resources in your marriage. Are you open to seeking professional guidance and support when needed? What is holding you back from doing so?

PRACTICE GRATITUDE

> *Cultivate an attitude of gratitude towards each other. Express appreciation for the little things, and never take each other's love and efforts for granted.*

Conclusion

In the dawn of 2070, a new era unfolds with the promise of love, unity, and a voyage to distant worlds. On the crimson landscapes of Mars, the first wedding bells resonate, marking humanity's audacious leap into the cosmos—a testament to our unquenchable thirst for exploration and growth.

Meanwhile, back on Earth, a somber note reverberates. Amidst the marvels of progress and innovation, a cry for help echoes through the air. Marital breakdowns have become an epidemic, casting a shadow of disillusionment over the sacred institution of marriage. Mental health struggles born of these shattered unions haunt the souls of countless individuals.

Yet, in this juxtaposition of worlds, hope emerges—the guardians of harmonious unions. They are a new tribe, a testament to the enduring power of love, the keepers of a flame that refuses to flicker in the face of adversity. Their love story, unlike so many others, does not crumble; instead, it stands as a bastion of strength, a testament to the triumph of human connection.

In the age of flying cars, rocket trains, and ingenious inventions, these wise souls have discovered the most extraordinary invention of all—a love that thrives and grows stronger with time. They are the living embodiment of the top habits of highly effective couples, a roadmap to bliss in an otherwise chaotic world.

Their journey has been one of storms and refinement, of trials that have forged them into unbreakable bonds of affection. They hold the secrets to building marriages that withstand the test of time, marriages that are not mere unions but sanctuaries of love and understanding.

In a world veiled in confusion, these exceptional couples shine as beacons of clarity and serenity. They have become the lodestars, guiding the lost ships of relationships toward safe harbors of happiness and fulfillment. The entire world looks up to them, for in their wisdom lies the elixir of harmonious existence. But the odyssey to becoming this blissful tribe doesn't commence in 2070x; it starts right here and now, with those who hold this book and have journeyed through its pages. As Dr. Joe Dispenza wisely noted, "Your personality determines your reality." Your marriage, your union, your love story—it will ultimately take the shape of your personality.

So, whether you stand amidst the chaos of a troubled marriage or embark on the threshold of a new one, know this: the state of your marriage mirrors the state of your being. The path to a blissful union, to becoming a part of this extraordinary tribe, begins with the commitment to work on yourself. As you transform, so too will your marriage, and together, you shall author a love story that defies the tides of time—a love story for the ages, etched in the annals of human history.

Everything We Call Bad Marriage Is Simply:

1. Ignorance of self – Indeed, understanding oneself and how

one has evolved over time is a crucial aspect of building a healthy and successful marriage. Self-awareness can help individuals identify their needs, values, and expectations, which are essential in fostering a strong and harmonious relationship with a partner.

When couples are aware of their own strengths and weaknesses, they can work together to overcome challenges and grow together. Ignorance of oneself can lead to misunderstandings, conflicts, and unmet expectations, which can strain a marriage. Therefore, self-awareness and continuous self-improvement are key components of a successful partnership.

2. Ignorance of your spouse– Understanding one's spouse is equally vital in creating a healthy and fulfilling marriage. Just as individuals change and evolve over time, so do their partners. Ignorance of your spouse's true self, including their values, desires, and personal growth, can lead to misunderstandings and conflicts in the relationship. It's essential for couples to continuously learn about each other, communicate openly, and be receptive to the changes that naturally occur in each person's life journey. By doing so, couples can strengthen their connection and build a lasting and loving partnership based on mutual understanding and acceptance.

3. Ignorance of marriage– Ignorance about the true nature and purpose of marriage can lead to misunderstandings, unmet expectations, and conflicts within a relationship. When couples enter into marriage without a clear understanding of what it entails, they may have unrealistic beliefs about the roles and responsibilities of each partner, the nature of love, or the challenges they may face together.

Marriage is more than just a legal contract or a societal norm. It's a profound and dynamic partnership that requires ongoing effort, growth, and adaptation from both individuals.

Understanding that marriage involves shared goals, mutual support, and a commitment to facing life's ups and downs together is crucial. It's about nurturing love, trust, and respect, and continuously working on maintaining a strong connection with your partner.

When couples are ignorant of these essential aspects of marriage, they may struggle to navigate the complexities of married life. Communication breaks down, conflicts escalate, and the relationship can become strained. However, with the right knowledge, willingness to learn and grow, and a commitment to understanding one another, couples can transform their marriage into a fulfilling and harmonious partnership.

Ultimately, addressing these forms of ignorance and actively seeking to understand oneself, one's partner and the institution of marriage can pave the way for a more meaningful and successful union. Couples who embark on this journey of selfdiscovery and shared understanding are better equipped to build a resilient and loving marriage that stands the test of time. 4. Ignorance of the building techniques– Ignorance of the building techniques in a marriage, or having shallow marital knowledge can indeed lead to difficulties within the relationship.

Just like constructing a sturdy building requires a deep understanding of architecture, engineering, and construction techniques, building a strong and lasting marriage demands knowledge and skills. Many couples enter marriage with limited knowledge of what it takes to nurture a healthy relationship.

They might not have learned effective communication, conflict resolution, or emotional intelligence skills. This lack of knowledge can hinder their ability to navigate the challenges that inevitably arise in any marriage. To overcome this form of ignorance, couples can invest in acquiring the necessary tools and knowledge to build a thriving partnership. This may involve seeking advice from experienced couples, attending marriage counseling or workshops, reading books on relationships, or even participating in online courses.

The goal is to deepen their understanding of each other and the dynamics of marriage. In essence, just as an architect studies blueprints and construction techniques to build a stable structure, couples can study and apply the principles and techniques that foster a strong and resilient marriage. This knowledge equips them to handle conflicts, communicate effectively, and nurture love and intimacy over time. It's an ongoing process of learning and growing together to create a harmonious and enduring
partnership.

5. Ignorance of your marital enemies– Understanding and identifying potential marital enemies is crucial for maintaining a healthy and thriving relationship. Ignorance of these enemies can indeed lead to unintentional sabotage of marital wellness.

Let's Explore This Concept Further:

In the journey of marriage, there are often unseen or overlooked adversaries that can undermine the strength and happiness of the union. These marital enemies can take various forms, such as:

A. Communication Breakdown: Poor communication or misunderstandings can gradually erode the trust and emotional connection between spouses. Ignoring the importance of effective communication can be a significant enemy of marital harmony.

B. Unresolved Conflicts: Every relationship faces conflicts, but failing to address and resolve them can allow bitterness and resentment to build over time. Ignoring the need for conflict resolution skills can be detrimental.

C. Lack of Intimacy: Emotional and physical intimacy are essential components of a successful marriage. Ignoring these aspects can lead to feelings of neglect or unmet needs, which can be damaging.

D. Financial Stress: Money-related issues are a common source of marital discord. Failing to manage finances effectively and discuss financial goals can strain the relationship.

E. Outside Influences: Interference from family, friends, or other external factors can create tension within a marriage. Ignoring boundaries and failing to protect the relationship from undue influences can be harmful.

F. Infidelity: Trust is the bedrock of any marriage, and infidelity can shatter it. Ignoring the potential for infidelity or not addressing trust issues can be a grave mistake.

G. Neglecting Self-Care: Both partners must prioritize selfcare to bring their best selves to the marriage. Ignoring selfcare can lead to burnout and neglect of the relationship.

H. Emotional Baggage: Unresolved emotional issues from the past can affect the present relationship. Ignoring the need for healing and personal growth can hinder marital happiness.

Recognizing these potential enemies and proactively addressing them is essential for a successful marriage. Couples can do this by investing time and effort in building emotional intelligence, seeking professional help when needed, setting healthy boundaries, and continuously nurturing their connection. Ignorance of these marital enemies can indeed sabotage marital wellness. However, by acknowledging and addressing these challenges, couples can strengthen their bond and fortify their marriage against potential threats, fostering a relationship that stands the test of time. In every corner of the world, beneath different skies and among diverse cultures, I've stood before eager audiences, sharing the light of marital wisdom. My purpose has always been clear: to bestow upon others the gift of illumination, to set their hearts free, and to ignite the flames of genuine happiness.

I've woven a definition of happiness: it's the beautiful process of embracing oneself fully, of creating and cherishing the celestial haven within, a sanctuary so powerful that the inferno of the external world can never extinguish its brilliance.

My mission, dear readers, transcends borders and transcends time. It's a quest to forge a tribe, a tribe that aspires to be the most remarkable, the most effective of its kind on this magnificent planet. Together, we shall radiate a profound light, one that guides not just our own footsteps but illuminates a path for others to follow.

In this world, where chaos often seems to reign, we seek to provide a clear beacon, a luminous guide for those yearning to thrive in the arms of joy. And we extend our loving hands to those who bear the weight of suffering, for through our collective wisdom, we shall bring the gentle touch of healing.

Today, you stand at the crossroads of destiny. You can choose to seize your own happiness by confronting your inner demons, by peeling away the layers of personal trauma. You can embark on a journey of profound self-discovery and healing, mastering the sacred habits that pave the way to an enduring family.

Within the depths of your being, you possess the potential to become the finest version of yourself, love, and strength. The time is now, dear friend. It is your moment to rise, to cultivate a family that is not just functional but a source of profound connection, warmth, and understanding.

With every sunrise, with every heartbeat, your destiny unfolds before you. In your hands, you can craft a family that not only endures but flourishes, a family that stands as a testament to the beauty of love and the resilience of the human spirit.

Arise, then, and embrace this calling. Join us on this incredible voyage towards a family that works, toward a world where love reigns supreme, and where each of us shines as a unique and radiant star in the boundless constellation of human existence.

CHOOSE LOVE
EVERY DAY

Love is a choice that you make every single day. Choose to love, honor, and cherish each other through the highs and lows, knowing that your commitment will keep you unbroken.

Write your new Love Philosophy here

Praise Fowowe is a leading expert in family life and relationship coaching. I've witnessed his ability to help countless families reconnect and find happiness, breaking down barriers to unity. His upcoming book, **UNBROKEN:** How Couples Can Build Marriages That Last Forever, is set to be an essential guide for couples everywhere, offering valuable insights and strategies for lasting relationships.

— **Remi Dairo,** CEO, Productivate Plus.

When I think of family life success, I think Praise Fowowe. This book is sure to be a blessing to you

— **Jimi Tewe**

Your consistent and insightful writing on marriage and the family system is truly commendable. Each piece reflects a deep understanding of these fundamental aspects of life, offering valuable perspectives that resonate with readers. Keep up the great work!

— **Dr Babajide**

Praise Fowowe is a beacon of hope for families, turning challenges into triumphs and transforming homes into sanctuaries of love. His teachings, deeply rooted in his own life experiences, offer couples the keys to harmony and fulfillment. In this book, Praise shares the
timeless principles that can elevate any relationship to new heights.

— **Bankole Williams**

For permissions requests, and enquiries about
UNBROKEN WORKSHOPS

Contact:
email:
admin@praisefowowedtech.com

Tel:
+234 708 654 9834
+44 7960 813430
+18178817269

Website:
www.praisefowowedtech.com/unbroken

OTHER RESOURCES
by Praise Fowowe Research

1. Out of the box parenting
2. Strictly for wives
3. Strictly for parents
4. Strictly for boys
5. Strictly for girls
6. New Ancestors VIP community
7. Human Engineering Programming
8. Oyela psychometric app for marital diagnostics

Within the depths of your being, you possess the potential to become the finest version of yourself, love, and strength. The time is now, dear friend. It is your moment to rise, to cultivate a family that is not just functional but a source of profound connection, warmth, and understanding.

With every sunrise, with every heartbeat, your destiny unfolds before you. In your hands, you can craft a family that not only endures but flourishes, a family that stands as a testament to the beauty of love and the resilience of the human spirit.

Arise, and embrace this calling.
Join us on this incredible voyage toward a family that works, toward a world where love reigns supreme, and where each of us shines as a unique and radiant star in the boundless constellation of human existence.

Meet the Author

Praise Fowowe is widely recognized as a global authority in Family Strategy and Innovation. With over two decades of pioneering family life solutions across Africa, the United Kingdom, and North America, Praise has distinguished himself as a sought-after keynote speaker, lecturer, trainer, advisor, researcher, and consultant. His groundbreaking work in Family Systems Engineering—a comprehensive framework for transforming families and communities—has received widespread acclaim from scholars and practitioners worldwide.

As a consultant to governments and organizations, Praise's insights and methodologies have shaped policies and practices that positively influence countless lives. His contributions have solidified his reputation as one of the most influential family life consultants globally. Currently, Praise lectures at the Institute of Family Engineering and Development, where he continues to drive innovation in the field.

Praise is married to Oluwatosin, and together, they are blessed with two children, David and Charis.

www.ingramcontent.com/pod-product-compliance
Lightning Source LLC
Chambersburg PA
CBHW020922160726
47993CB00005B/2089